T0278329

THE
RUMBLING
EARTH

THE
RUMBLING
EARTH

THE STORY
OF INDIAN
EARTHQUAKES

C.P. RAJENDRAN
KUSALA RAJENDRAN

VINTAGE

An imprint of Penguin Random House

VINTAGE

USA | Canada | UK | Ireland | Australia
New Zealand | India | South Africa | China | Singapore

Vintage is part of the Penguin Random House group of companies
whose addresses can be found at global.penguinrandomhouse.com

Published by Penguin Random House India Pvt. Ltd
4th Floor, Capital Tower 1, MG Road,
Gurugram 122 002, Haryana, India

First published in Vintage by Penguin Random House India 2024

ISBN 9780670095612

Typeset in Sabon by MAP Systems, Bengaluru, India
Printed at Thomson Press India Ltd, New Delhi

www.penguin.co.in

*To our parents and teachers, who
showed us the less-trodden paths*

Contents

Foreword

Earthquakes are the most frightening natural hazard. They often occur with no warning of any sort and kill as many as 50,000 people within seconds when buildings collapse. In most parts of the world, they are sufficiently infrequent; there is little incentive for either politicians or the public to worry about enforcing seismic building codes. This problem, which lies at the heart of the recent earthquake disasters in Turkey and elsewhere, is why I hope this book will be widely read.

The authors have made an extraordinary collection of first-hand accounts of earthquakes and tsunamis. My favourite is the story of Tilly Smith, a ten-year-old girl from the UK who was in Phuket with her mother. She remembered learning about tsunamis from her geography teacher and realized one was arriving. Her presence of mind saved the lives of over hundred people, including herself and her mother. This story shows the great importance of teaching children about the danger of earthquakes and collapsing buildings. They will take this knowledge home and educate their parents. This book, which is both entertaining and educational, with panels explaining how plate motions and faults combine to produce such terrible destruction, is exactly what is needed.

We now understand how earthquakes are produced, by the slow movement of plates. However, when I was an undergraduate in 1960, some seismologists still believed that earthquakes were produced by some sort of explosion or phase change. It was also quite unclear why earthquakes occurred in long linear belts. With the discovery of plate tectonics in 1966, these issues (and many others) had obvious explanations. Indeed, the resulting theory remains one of the easiest parts of geology to teach students and has even caused politicians to talk about 'the movement of tectonic plates'! I was extremely lucky to be involved: I had just finished my PhD and had a fellowship that supported me for three years to do whatever interested me. When Jason Morgan and I discovered plate tectonics, as the collection of ideas that we proposed in 1966 is now known, I knew rather little about earthquake seismology. The authors of this book have made this rather technical subject interesting and accessible to a wide audience by collecting an extraordinary variety of first-hand accounts.

I strongly recommend it.

18 May 2023   Dan McKenzie
                                     Professor of geophysics
                                      Cambridge University

Preface

What made us work on a book on Indian earthquakes and the related geological processes meant for public understanding? That needs some elaboration. Let us start with a fundamental problem in our science education—that Earth science is barely considered a science subject in our curriculum. This is not a problem confined to India but is universally felt. In her article titled 'Americans are missing a key stratum of modern knowledge', Kendra Pierre-Louis, a science reporter with an educational background in Earth science, expresses her anguish about these topics being ignored in high schools and junior colleges.[1] It is time our science education is restructured so that Earth science gets its due, at par with the status enjoyed by physics, biology and chemistry. She argues that the subject needs serious attention, especially with the background of a possible dystopian future awaiting humanity in the form of global warming and its impacts on our climate. The global hazards of climate change are ever-expanding, and an understanding of these processes is deeply grounded in Earth science. The threats to air, water, soil and land fundamentally impact human existence, to list a few. Humanity is beginning to realize the growing threat of such hazards and the enormity of these challenges.

There is much Earth science can offer as solutions to this unprecedented existential crisis facing humanity.

The efforts also call for an urgent need to popularize Earth science and educate students to gain a minimum scientific literacy in various branches of Earth science. Events like TierraFest, held every year in Mexico City, give us much hope. Worth emulating by communities in other parts of the world, this annual interactive event that challenges 'the traditional vertical model of science communication' facilitates scientists in sharing knowledge about Earth sciences and the environment with the public.[2] Equally commendable are the initiatives taken by the Earth scientists who are raising awareness about the hazards associated with Mount Nyiragongo in Congo. Lava flow from this active volcano, considered one of the most dangerous in the world, flooded the outskirts of the city of Goma in May 2021.[3] Such exceptional public-outreach efforts have also been reported from India. The Society of Earth Scientists based in Lucknow has been championing the cause of protecting India's unique geological sites and fossils for posterity. In Hyderabad, the Society to Save Rocks, formed by a group of artists, photographers and environmentalists, has been doing a great service for the last twenty-five years by conducting awareness programmes to save the unique, rocky landscape of the city and its surroundings against real-estate interests.

A knowledge base at the community level would help people make sense of the environmental changes and the hazards they are exposed to. An understanding of the concepts of Earth science would also help people cope with various natural hazards and lessen their impacts. For example, awareness of plate tectonics, generation of earthquakes and their impact on buildings would help people make assessments about their environment. Earth science practitioners must take up the task of sensitizing the community about new developments in the field and their implications for environmental stability. Society at large should be able to make intelligent choices and devise newer ways of using Earth science in everyday planning and decision-making, especially in the areas of hazard mitigation, shrinking groundwater, increased water degradation and toxic waste management. Consider the plan to dispose of the high-level radioactive waste under Yucca Mountain, in the Nevada desert, a project approved by the US in 2002. The scientific case for Yucca Mountain as a waste repository located in the sparsely populated desert state of Nevada was seemingly sound—a prognosis that was arrived at after more than thirty years of geological study.[4] Contested by the public, the project had to be shelved pending the final decision from the US Nuclear Regulatory Commission, a decision that critics allege has more to do with politics than science. Such critical issues will keep coming up and environmentally sensitive projects will require constant attention and advice from Earth scientists to help communities make prudent decisions.

Earthquakes, which top the list of natural hazards, form the subject matter of this book. This book on Indian earthquakes, interspersed with vignettes from our own professional journey, is a step in a direction that would assist in popularizing Earth sciences. Much of our academic research is centred on furthering the scientific understanding of earthquakes that have occurred in the Indian subcontinent. Writing this book also reflects our belief that science writing with a goal of attaining a wider readership has a place in modern book publishing. We hope this publication will also be useful for teachers in high schools and colleges as a teaching aid.

We appreciate the efforts of the associate publisher, Elizabeth Kuruvilla, at Penguin Random House India, in overseeing the completion of this project and Saba Nehal for copy-editing it. We are thankful to our colleagues and peers at the Indian Institute of Science, National Institute of Advanced Studies and Jawaharlal Nehru Centre for Advanced Scientific Research, all located in Bengaluru, for their support. In particular, we thank Debasish Roy for his support. Student associate Swapnil Mache, currently at the University of Twente, Netherlands, was of great help in editing the figures and sometimes redrafting them. Revathy Parameswaran, who is conducting research in earthquake science at the University of Alaska, helped with some of the beautiful sketches. Jaishri Sanwal of the Jawaharlal Nehru Centre was supportive in various ways during the preparation of this book. Roger Bilham, who has conducted many studies on earthquakes around the world, including India, has been a constant source of inspiration and his constructive feedback on our work was very helpful. He read through the entire draft and offered several valuable suggestions that improved the contents of this book. The final editing of this book was done during the spring of 2023 at Higganum, Connecticut, USA, while we were setting up the non-profit Consortium for Sustainable Development. We were hosted by Murale Gopinathan, a long-time friend and the president of the consortium. A special word of gratitude to Pradeep Talwani for his mentorship at the University of South Carolina and for introducing us to the exciting field of earthquake research. Dan McKenzie, the originator of the theory of plate tectonics that revolutionized Earth science, wrote the foreword to his book. We are grateful to him for having gone through the manuscript and providing an apt introduction for this book. Coming from a legend in Earth sciences, we consider his gesture an honour. Our final words of thanks are reserved for our fellow backpackers for their company in our long and arduous professional journey. And, of course, to our family members, including our son Rahul, his wife Divya (Abhirami) and their daughter Kalki, for their tolerance and forgiveness, and their help in keeping the work–life balance stable despite lapses from our side.

18 May 2023
C.P. Rajendran
Kusala Rajendran

Chapter 1

When the Earth Shakes

A bad earthquake at once destroys the oldest associations: the world, the very emblem of all that is solid, has moved beneath our feet like a crust over a fluid; one second of time has conveyed to the mind a strange idea of insecurity, which hours of reflection would never have created.

—*Charles Darwin*[*]

An earthquake of magnitude (M_w) 4.5 with its epicentre at a far-flung location would hardly be noticed by anyone except those who make routine entries of global earthquakes. Global earthquake monitoring agencies report that about 1500 earthquakes of magnitude 5 occur yearly.[1] Many of them take place under the oceans or in uninhabited regions:

---

[*] Charles Darwin experienced a major earthquake in the Concepción-Valdivia region of Chile in February 1835, popularly known as Darwin's earthquake later. His observations dramatically illustrated the geologic principles of James Hutton and Charles Lyell which maintained that the surface of the Earth was subject to alterations by natural events, such as earthquakes, volcanoes and the erosive action of wind and water, operating over very long periods of time.

forests, deserts or mountains. Occasionally, they also strike densely populated areas, and that is when they cause fear and panic. One such event happened near New Delhi on 29 May 2020. A few minutes past nine in the night, a magnitude 4.5 earthquake jolted the city's residents. The epicentre was near Rohtak in Haryana, about 70 km north-west of New Delhi. The tremors were felt in and around Delhi, most notably in the urban centres of Noida and Gurugram. Located on the outskirts of Delhi, these cities are known for their posh commercial outlets and high-rise buildings. Here, the residents reported that the ground shook vigorously for about six to seven seconds, and most of them, especially those in the high-rises, ran out of their homes when they felt the shaking.

Experiencing an earthquake of mild (3–3.9) to moderate (5–5.9) magnitude is not new for the residents of Delhi. The recent history of Delhi is replete with such low-intensity earthquakes. The residents may know that Delhi is on the outskirts of one of the most seismically active mountains in the world—the Himalayas. Several destructive earthquakes have occurred in the Himalayas in the past. In 1803, an earthquake of magnitude ~7.5 near Uttarkashi in the Garhwal Himalayas, about 450 km north of Delhi, caused some damage to the Qutb Minar. The moderate earthquakes that rocked Uttarkashi in 1991 (M_w 6.8) and Chamoli in 1999 (M_w 6.6) remind the residents of Delhi about the potential threats lurking under the Garhwal and Kumaun Himalayas with ramifications for the north Indian plains.

The Chamoli earthquake in the eastern part of the Garhwal Himalayas was a tutorial for all those who took part in the post-earthquake surveys. Although the earthquake was about 300 km north of Delhi, it minimally affected some areas in the capital city. The ground shaking led to minor cracks in some houses in the Yamuna plains. The damage potential would increase exponentially with an uptick in magnitude. Take the case of the earthquake in 1905 (M_w 7.8) in the Kangra Valley, in north-west India, about 500 km from Delhi. This earthquake is perhaps the largest to have been felt in Delhi in the last century. The destruction in the areas close to its source was total, and thousands lost their lives. There have been several reminders of the existence such active sources in the Himalayas in the form of small and moderate earthquakes in recent years, felt by the residents of Delhi and other north Indian cities, towns and villages.

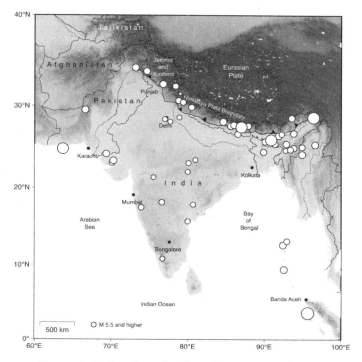

Figure 1.1: Earthquake distribution in India and adjacent areas since historic times.

An Unusual Calm

It is not just the Indian part of the Himalayas, earthquakes from faraway places such as the Afghanistan–Tajikistan border can also rock Delhi and nearby cities. On 5 February 2022, an earthquake of magnitude 5.7 from the Afghanistan–Tajikistan border sent shock waves through many parts of northern India. Some residents of Noida, on the outskirts of Delhi, felt the ground shake for at least twenty seconds. According to the Indian TV channel NDTV, Shashank Singh, a resident of Noida, reported on 5 February: 'I thought my head was spinning and started to shut my eyes when suddenly I looked at the fan and realized it's an earthquake. Strong tremors were felt for about 25–30 seconds in Noida.' These are smaller events, but others could be deadly at their sources and quite shaky at distant locations such as Delhi.

Residents of north Indian cities often recall their experience on 8 October 2005, when a deadly earthquake of magnitude (M_w 7.6) rocked the part of Kashmir on the Pakistan side of the Line of Control. The official death toll was 79,000 from Pakistan-occupied Kashmir and the Northwest Frontier Province.[2] The Indian side reported a death toll of more than 1300 people.[3] Exacerbated mainly by poor construction, this huge death toll was unprecedented for any modern-day Himalayan earthquake. The tremors were felt up to a distance of 1000 km from the epicentre, as far away as Punjab in northern India. It was a demonstration that the alluvial soil can amplify the energy content of the earthquake waves and effects can be felt at far away locations. The effect would be felt more in high-rise buildings. Given such experiences, those living in the Ganga Basin are aware of the peculiarities of their ground.

Most people know that the real danger is from the Himalayas. Although the Himalayas are known for devastating earthquakes, they have maintained an unusual calm over the last seventy years. With the possibility of a significant future earthquake in the Himalayas, even some mild shocks are suspected as forerunners. Before the 29 May 2020 earthquake near Delhi, the National Centre for Seismology (NCS) had recorded a few small tremors since 12 April the same year, as documented in one of its research publications.[4] Can the small tremors be taken as potential precursors of an impending larger earthquake? Some would argue, based on examples, that earthquakes rarely give any detectable precursors or indications as warnings. Perhaps an exhaustive search of the global earthquake catalogue would point to a few exceptions where foreshocks have been detected but recognized only after the main earthquake. From India, there is the example of the 1993 Killari (Latur, Maharashtra) earthquake, which was preceded by small shocks, but these were not recognized as foreshocks. The seismological observatory at the National Geophysical Research Institute at Hyderabad recorded twenty-six shocks of magnitude 2–4 from the Killari region in 1992. Still, they were not recognized as foreshocks until the 6.3 earthquake occurred in September 1993. There are many instances where a mild shock passes off without leading to anything significant, such as the Rohtak earthquake of 29 May 2020, near Delhi. And, of course, there are numerous examples of large earthquakes that occur with no sign of foreshocks. Therefore, global studies on earthquake patterns have not identified any discernible pattern to predict a main earthquake using smaller shocks that precede them.

As multiple and contradicting ideas appeared in the public domain after the 29 May earthquake, panic and confusion built among the people. Another earthquake of magnitude 2.7 shook Delhi on 22 March 2023. This followed the magnitude 6.6 earthquake in Afghanistan on 21 March that was felt in many Indian cities including Delhi, causing a lot of concern. The most frequent question raised in the context of the Delhi earthquake was whether the minor event was a precursor to a larger one. Was it a wake-up call? As scientists with a research background in the Himalayan earthquakes, we also had to answer several queries, including those raised by the media. Interacting with the general public on earthquakes is something we have been doing for over three decades. However, we have learned that each region and every earthquake pose different challenges. A difficult one that we had to deal with was the moderate earthquake that occurred in Killari, in September 1993. Tectonically stable and generally free of earthquakes, this region was considered 'aseismic'. Therefore, the question was, why did an earthquake occur here in the first place? The earthquake (M_w 7.7) that occurred in Bhuj on 26 January 2001 was equally challenging to explain to the general public. The question at that time was why a large earthquake occurred just about 200 years after a similar event—in 1819—in the same region, and why buildings collapsed only in some regions.

Public Outreach

Why do scientists fail to predict earthquakes while they succeed in predicting events like cyclones? It has been quite hard to explain why earthquake prediction is tough while conversing with the general public. There is no available technology which allows scientists to predict the time, location and magnitude of an impending earthquake with such efficacy that people can be evacuated to safety. Conversing on earthquake prediction has turned out to be not just difficult but also a personal risk for seismologists sometimes. This predicament became apparent from the experience of the six Italian scientists who were sentenced to a six-year prison term for their statements before an earthquake in the town of L'Aquila. They were convicted for downplaying the possible risk from a series of tremors culminating in a magnitude 6.3 quake on 6 April 2009 which killed 309 people.[5] The manslaughter conviction was overturned later. Incidents such as this have the potential to create a trust deficit between the administration and the scientists. How often do small tremors lead to significant earthquakes? What if the predictions turn out to be wrong? There could be social and economic consequences. What if the scientists' statements lead to a false sense of security, leading to disastrous outcomes even when people follow the scientific advisory, as in L'Aquila? The predicament of earthquake scientists interacting with the common public and government authorities is not enviable.

Back in Kerala, we faced such a challenging situation. An earthquake of magnitude 4.3 hit a highly populated village near Wadakkancheri, 30 km north of Thrissur in central Kerala, on 4 December 1994. With its focus at a depth of less than 10 km, the earthquake was not particularly damaging, except for some poorly engineered houses. What was alarming was the long sequence of aftershocks that occurred for several weeks, their number nearing 100 in a matter of a few weeks. This was a first-time experience for people in that area. What made the situation worse were the thundering sounds that accompanied these shallow-focus shocks. The residents described that the ground vibrated as if a train was passing beneath it. The situation became so alarming that many people moved to tents in open fields. The Wadakkancheri earthquake occurred a year after the earthquake (M_w 6.3) in Killari (Latur), which killed more than 10,000 people and demolished almost every house in that village. A region placed in Zone I of the then seismic zonation map of India (it has since been changed), Latur and its neighbourhood was considered as a region of the least seismic activity and the lowest expectancy of any damaging earthquakes.

Could a Killari-like earthquake occur in this small village in north Kerala? Were the smaller shocks the foreshocks to a larger earthquake? Scientists have to find answers to such questions when they interact with the common people. A definitive answer was not possible in this case, but we tried to explain why a large earthquake was unlikely to happen in India's stable peninsular shield region. We reminded the local people that the houses that had collapsed in the 1993 Killari earthquake were non-engineered adobes built in clay and rocks. We told them that the shocks in Wadakkancheri were getting fewer in number and the sequence was waning. Such a situation was unlikely to progress to a larger-magnitude earthquake, we tried to convince them. As time proved, that was indeed the case. Perhaps it was less risky to make that postulation in a region that was less active seismically, located far away from active faults that have histories of large earthquakes.

Eventful Decades

The last three decades have been quite eventful in the earthquake history of India and the subcontinent. There were many destructive earthquakes—Killari (1993), Jabalpur (1998), Chamoli (1999), Bhuj (2001), Kashmir (2005) and Nepal (2015). Then there was the great earthquake of 2004 that originated off the coast of Sumatra and caused an unprecedented tsunami. The earthquake and the tsunami caused extensive damage to property and led to permanent changes in the landscape of the Andaman and Nicobar Islands. Uplift and subsidence of land[†] were noted in many regions along the Andaman and Nicobar Islands. Many parts of eastern Port Blair sank by about 1 metre, whereas the western Sentinel Island rose by 1 metre. The southern tip of Car Nicobar subsided by about 3 metres. The earthquake devastated the Andaman and Nicobar Islands, both due to the earthquake and the tsunami that followed. The fault rupture[‡] created by the 2004 earthquake was about 1300 km long, and extended to depths up to 24 km. The transoceanic tsunami generated by the rupture travelled to almost every Indian Ocean rim country. Much of the south-eastern coast and some parts of the west coast of India were severely affected. Several thousands of lives were lost. And with this, Indian earthquake scientists had a new challenge to deal with—the hitherto under-recognized hazard of tsunamis.

* * *

[†] Such phenomena are common for large earthquakes. Uplift refers to the rising of portions of the Earth's surface while sinking of land refers to the downward shift of portions of Earth's surface. Both uplift and sinking can be due to plate tectonic movements.

[‡] Great earthquakes create fault ruptures due to the movement on faults deep within the earth. Surface ruptures created this way may extend from a few to hundreds of kilometres, based on the size and the nature of the earthquake. Ruptures created by some earthquakes may terminate before reaching the surface. Fault ruptures expressed on the surface are very useful for scientists to map the causative fault and infer more direct information about the earthquake.

Earthquake Parameters

The main parameters of studying an earthquake are its hypocentre or focus, epicentre, time of origin and magnitude. The point of origin of the earthquake is called the focus or hypocentre. Epicentre is the point on the Earth's surface directly above with its coordinates given in units of latitude and longitude. Focal depth is the depth to the focus, (classified as shallow: 0–70 km; intermediate: 70–300 km; and deep: 300–700 km). The severity of the earthquake depends on its energy release, indicated using two measures—magnitude and intensity. **Magnitude** is a measure of its energy, as estimated from the amplitude of waves caused by the motion of particles which are transmitted as seismic waves. Amplitude of the seismic wave is a measure the maximum displacement of the particle motions, or the recorded height of the ripple crest of the seismic wave. The stronger the earthquake, the larger will be the amplitude of the seismic wave. Charles Richter, an American seismologist, introduced the concept of magnitude in the 1930s. He used the distance between the seismograph and the epicentre and the maximum amplitude of the seismic wave to express magnitude (M). An earthquake of magnitude 1.5 is considered small, and one of 8 is classified as great. Magnitude is also determined using body waves (Mb) and surface waves (Ms). Body waves (P and S) travel through the Earth's interior, P being the first to reach, followed by S. Surface waves (Love waves, Rayleigh waves) are of lower frequency and travel slower along the surface of the Earth. Moment magnitude (M_w), based on the modelling of seismic waves, is a more precise representation as it incorporates the length and width the fault. For historical earthquakes, magnitude is usually estimated from intensity reports and field evidence of the fault. Thus, modern-day magnitude estimates use the symbol M_w. Other symbols are also used in this book, based on their original method of estimation. While the magnitude of an earthquake does not vary with location, **Intensity**, which describes an earthquake using its observed effects, varies from place to place. Regions of equal intensity are represented by isoseismals. Modified Mercalli (MM) Intensity Scale and the Medvedev-Sponhener-Karnik (MSK) Intensity Scale are the most commonly used. These scales usually provides ten or twelve grades starting with most feeble vibrations (I), and going up to most violent (XII) (i.e., total destruction).

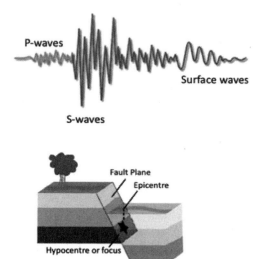

Figure 1.2: (Top) *A representative seismogram showing P, S and Surface waves.* (Bottom) *Parameters of an earthquake.*

Chapter 2

Our Tryst with Earthquakes

Much as I admired the elegance of physical theories, which at that time geology wholly lacked, I preferred a life in the woods to one in the laboratory.
                                            —*J. Tuzo Wilson*

Writing about earthquakes involves going through our lives together for more than four decades. Coming from families with different socio-political, educational and cultural backgrounds, a career in Earth science was more by chance rather than by choice. But that chance opened windows of opportunities and brought a geologist and geophysicist together in a tryst with earthquakes. Our respective training in geology (C.P. Rajendran) and applied geophysics (Kusala Rajendran) made it possible for us to look at earthquakes through a wider lens. A love for history was advantageous as we dug for information on past earthquakes. Our quest to study earthquakes and tsunamis has taken us around the globe, and these journeys allowed us to meet and work with pioneers in earthquake and tsunami research.

In 1988, we moved to the US for doctoral and post-doctoral studies from the Centre for Earth Science Studies, a state-funded research organization in Kerala at that time. We were at the right place and at the right time. Joining the Department of Geological Sciences at the University of South Carolina from 1988 to 1993 was a fortuitous opportunity. The late 1980s and 1990s saw the widespread application of paleoseismology,[*] the science of studying earthquakes using geological evidence as a powerful tool. It could be used to understand the behaviour of faults, particularly to find out how they evolved. Our tryst with earthquakes began in the beautiful town of Charleston on the Atlantic Coast in the state of South Carolina. We were in proximity to the source zone of the 1886 Charleston earthquake (M_w 7.3), the most significant event to have occurred since historical times. We wanted to know how this earthquake originated under this historical town, known

---

[*] Paleoseismology is the science that reconstructs the history of earthquake activity long before instrumental recording began. The possibility of reconstructing earthquakes was noted in the 1880s, when G.K. Gilbert, an American geologist, first found the repetitive features of major earthquakes along the Wasatch fault in the United States. Its development as a modern science started in the 1970s, when Kerry Sieh, the famous Caltech-based earth scientist, used the idea to study the ancient history of the San Andreas fault. Since then, it has been used to unravel the history of many earthquakes. The basic idea is that when an earthquake occurs along a fault, the layers are disrupted, broken and deformed. As time goes by, new layers are deposited and the disrupted layer is preserved. If this layer can be revealed through trenching excavations to expose the fault, a timeline can be worked out backwards by dating the various layers.

for its iconic antebellum houses and roads lined with oaks dripping with Spanish moss, in the American South.

Earthquake scientists from the US Geological Survey and the geological sciences department relied on techniques in paleoseismology—the new tool in finding geological evidence for any earthquakes that must have occurred near the source of the 1886 earthquake. We (mostly CP) were lucky to join this exciting effort. CP joined the team led by Pradeep Talwani, where he received the training to be an earthquake detective, one who hunts for ancient earthquakes. The geological search for the 1886 earthquake's predecessors took us to the vast expanses of Charleston's coastal swamp, often to be lost in its complex labyrinth of waterways. Here we found the clues of previous earthquakes in the form of sandblows, the result of soil liquefaction,[†] preserved in the sedimentary sections.

Our partnership, which started from Charleston, has taken us through Latur in central India, Bhuj in western Gujarat, Shillong and Arunachal Pradesh in the north-east, Nepal, and the Garhwal and Kumaun Himalayas. Searching for the geological archives of past tsunamis took us to Chile,

---

[†] Sandblows are formed by liquefaction, a process that leads to the loss of strength and stiffness of soil during an earthquake. As the granular structure of the soil collapses during the shaking, the density of the soil increases, and the increased pressure squeezes the water out of the pore spaces creating sandblows or sand boils. Due to the way in which water mixed with sand is ejected strongly, locals often refer to them as sand volcanoes. Sandblows have been observed in the aftermath of several large earthquakes. As the blow gets covered in future, it may preserve organic materials within its deposits. By digging into old sandblows, geologist can find their predecessors and date them, giving ideas about past earthquakes.

Alaska, Indonesia, Japan, Thailand, Iran and Sri Lanka. In India, the eastern coastal regions of the Indian mainland and the Andaman and Nicobar Islands was our turf. Our relocation to India's premier institutes (Kusala Rajendran to the Indian Institute of Science in 2007 and C.P. Rajendran to the Indian Institute of Science in 2008 and Jawaharlal Nehru Centre for Advanced Scientific Research in 2013) was most transformative in our academic endeavours, and working together as a geologist and seismologist pair was perhaps our USP.

Partnership in Seismology

Our return to India in 1993 coincided with the surprise earthquake near Latur (Killari) in Maharashtra. We were equipped with tools to take up earthquake studies at the time. Many historically documented great earthquakes have rocked India in the past centuries, from its north-eastern to north-western regions. With its relatively longer recorded history and ancient cultural archives, India was better placed for practising a host of tools—from paleoseismology to archaeoseismology[‡]— for tracking past earthquakes that might have struck these regions. The location of the 1819 earthquake in the Rann of Kutch in north-western India was our prime destination. But there was more to come and we became busy with many earthquakes that followed—

[‡] Archaeoseismology is the study of past earthquakes that have not been historically recorded. Archaeological sites often preserve destruction from past earthquakes which are missing from the historical records. It helps to bridge the gap between the well documented instrumental and historical seismology, and data derived from paleoseismology.

Latur, 1993, Jabalpur, 1998, Chamoli, 1999, Bhuj, 2001, Kashmir, 2005, Sikkim, 2011 and Nepal, 2015, among the significant ones. These were opportunities to observe and learn. These earthquakes have often been portrayed in scientific literature as outstanding examples of tectonic processes that helped scientists learn more about their causes and outcomes, as observed from the surface. And then there was the great earthquake of 2004 off the coast of Sumatra and the ensuing tsunami, a unique experience for the common public and the earth scientists in the South Asian countries.

The large twin earthquakes near Kathmandu, Nepal on 25 April and 12 May 2015 (M_w 7.6; 7.3) were the most recent. Accompanied by students, we climbed to the Siddha Gufa on the Prithvi Highway. The largest cave in Nepal and the second largest in Asia, the 0.5 km deep interior of this cave is decorated with impressive stalactites and stalagmites. Could the earthquake have shifted any of these structures? That could only be ascertained by walking into the dark and slippery interiors of the cave. Using our dim headlights, we surveyed the cave and found that the vertical growth of limestone deposits emerging from the ground and those growing down from the roof were intact. There were no signs of displacement or fresh breakage, an observation that was confirmed by the cave keeper. Sitting outside the cave and enjoying the panoramic view of the landscape that spreads to the distant hills, the cave keeper had not even felt the earthquake and came to know about it much later. He believed that while the buildings outside, including some ancient structures, had collapsed, killing many people, the cave was unaffected. He said he preferred to remain inside the safety of the cave in case another earthquake happened.

Figure 2.1: View of the Siddha Gufa cave in Nepal.

An earthquake once shook us on the salt marsh of Kutch. We were in the open, standing on muddy salt marsh, an area that we had been visiting since 1998 to study the signatures of the historically known 1819 earthquake. But during our visits, we had never felt any shaking. It was during the field study of the 26 January M_w 7.6 earthquake, that we really felt a quake that rocked the Rann. We were lucky to be accompanied by Arch Johnston from Memphis University, whose seminal papers on continental earthquakes described the 1819 earthquake of Kutch as one of the most fascinating historical events.[1] It was regarded as a special event because it was the first large earthquake in the continental interior region that caused a spectacular morphological feature—a nearly 90 km long mount that rose more than 4 m at some locations. The newly created mount (a scarp in geological terminology), named the Allah Bund, blocked the Nara (Puran) River, the eastern branch of the Indus River and formed a new lake. With the formation of such remarkable features, the earthquake found a place in the classic textbook,

Principles of Geology by Sir Charles Lyell, a British geologist.[2] Arch was fulfilling his lifelong desire to visit the salt plains of the Rann where the earthquake, oft-quoted in the annals of earthquake research, had occurred. Did he secretly wish to witness an earthquake in Kutch? Perhaps yes. On that hot afternoon, while standing in the white desert, where even the air tasted salty, the shaking almost knocked us down. It was not very scary, but the muddy salt platform on which we were standing was making a vibratory motion. We saw Arch struggling to balance his tall frame, yet clapping his hands and laughing aloud and shouting 'thank you'. Was he thanking us for bringing him there, or was he thanking the Earth for his once-in-a-lifetime experience of being shaken by an earthquake in the land he wrote about?

The spectacular land and the 1819 earthquake that Arch Johnston wrote about had brought us to Kutch. That is where we started our quest for the hidden trails of past earthquakes. Working at locations close to the 'Bund' that have mystified the region's residents for nearly two centuries, we found traces of its 900-year-old predecessor.[3] We were often surrounded by locals who were curious about us digging up the place to find evidence of ancient earthquakes. Conscious of the archaeological significance of the area, they would accompany us, often offering a helping hand and telling us that some fortune seekers had been lucky to retrieve gold ornaments and coins there. We did not find any gold but were fortunate to dig into the relics of a disturbed ancient settlement which we dated as 1000 CE, based on organic remains. We could ascribe it to the predecessor of the 1819 event i.e., an earthquake that occurred about 900 years before 1819. Interestingly, the same region was occupied by later settlers, and they had built a tax collection centre at that spot. The 1819 earthquake levelled that structure to a pile of bricks. That is where we got the evidence for two earthquakes stacked up in the same trench. Then there was the most recent earthquake of 26 January 2001, which devastated the cities of Bhuj and distant Ahmedabad and demonstrated what a large earthquake could do in a waterlogged marshland. An entire chapter in this book is devoted to these two earthquakes.

Earthquake Detectives

The year 1993 was important in our journey. In July, we returned to India to rejoin our positions at the Centre for Earth Sciences in Trivandrum, Kerala (now a National Centre). We had planned to raise research grants and start working in Kutch, a low-lying coastal region like Charleston. Both these places generated large earthquakes in the nineteenth century. What geologists describe as 'passive continental margins', these regions are considered to have greater potential to host earthquakes. Because of the availability of saturated sand horizons, these regions are highly prone to liquefaction. Exploring such regions could lead to the discovery of the vestiges of old earthquakes. Kutch also had a long-documented history of settlements that could offer additional evidence of earthquake-related destruction.

That is what one of us (CP) was trained to do, to hunt for older sandblows and other sedimentary features formed by ancient earthquakes and estimate their ages. We were getting ready to start our work in Kutch, when something else happened. Less than two months after we arrived in India, the Indian heartland was shaken by an earthquake in the early morning hours of 23 September. It was moderate but devastating, killing nearly 10,000 unsuspecting people who lived in the small village of Killari, near Latur, Maharashtra. The people who lived in the area had never experienced any earthquakes since historical times. The seismic zonation map of India had placed the region in Zone I, which had the least possibility of any earthquake. But when it happened, it reduced the houses to heaps of rubble. It was a testimony to the statement that buildings and not earthquakes kill people. The situation demanded attention, and, keeping the 1819 files on the back burner, we moved to Killari. Drawing parallels with studies by Anthony Crone of the US Geological Survey who studied similar earthquakes in Australia, we began our work in Killari. We explored the region to find evidence of any surface expressions of movement on the fault that caused the earthquake. In that flat and featureless basalt terrain, there was a subtle surface rupture that allowed us to explain the earthquake. We narrate that story in a chapter devoted to such mid-continental earthquakes. Earthquakes like the one in Killari are very dangerous, as they hit the least expected locations with no preparedness like a bolt from the sky.

The Lure of the Mountains

The Himalayas were beckoning. Plate tectonic theory had already demarcated the great Himalayan arc, marked not only by its topographic signature but also by moderate, large and great earthquakes since historical times. We were interested in finding out how frequently the Main Frontal Thrust (MFT)[§] in the central Himalayas gets ruptured

---

[§] The Main Frontal Thrust (MFT), also known as the Himalayan Frontal Thrust (HFT), is a geological fault trace in the Himalayas

in great earthquakes. Great and large earthquakes have occurred on the MFT—Uttarkashi, 1803; Kangra, 1905; Bihar–Nepal, 1934 among them. Each of these earthquakes have caused severe damage and loss of life in large areas. It is also noted that large parts of this great fault, especially in the central Himalaya have not caused any great earthquake for at least 500 years, if not longer. Any future earthquake on the MFT would be very damaging with much economic and societal implications. We first visited the Himalayas in 1999 to study the Chamoli earthquake that occurred in March of that year. Surveying of the earthquake-affected regions opened a new window for us—to use the age-old temples and other historical monuments as witnesses or victims of old earthquakes. We found evidence of damage from an earthquake in 1803 in the Gopeshwar Temple of Gopinath, near Chamoli.

Looking for evidence for past events, even an earthquake, requires the skills of a detective. At the Gopeshwar Temple (near Chamoli), the twelfth century CE (1191 CE) structure, located 5 km away from the epicentre of the Chamoli earthquake was only marginally affected. However, the temple walls displayed evidence, including overturned building stones, suggesting reconstruction. The inscriptions were interpreted as evidence for reconstruction after the temple was damaged in the 1803 earthquake. But to what extent was the damage? Did it just crack, or did it collapse? That would provide a clue to the strength of shaking. The temple priest was kind enough to take us to the

---

that defines the boundary between the Himalayan foothills and Indo-Gangetic plain. MFT is the youngest of the large thrust faults formed as a result of the convergence of India and Eurasian plates at the rate of 4 to 5 cm/year.

sanctum, where a reconstructed wall had used old bricks with discontinuous and sometimes inverted scriptures. This was clear evidence that the 1803 earthquake was strong enough to knock down the temple. The potential of using ancient temples with well-documented histories as indicators of ground shaking was promising. Now, we could apply the concepts of archaeoseismology to date ancient earthquakes of the Himalayas.

The theory of seismic gap[¶] was gaining attention by the 1980s as a concept that could help identify the locations of future earthquakes. The name 'seismic gap' might imply a long time interval between earthquakes, but in reality it implies gaps in space. Consider a plate boundary like the Himalayas where earthquakes occur during intervals of a few hundreds of years and release stresses. Each of these earthquakes might break a few hundreds of kilometres of the fault that marks the plate boundary. As the entire plate boundary is affected by plate motions, the unbroken patches are also under stress and they must also release the stresses at some point of time. Such segments are identified as potential locations of future earthquakes. In his seminal paper published in 1987, Kailash Khatri, a noted Indian seismologist, suggested that such gaps exist between locations of past great earthquakes in the Himalayas.[4] The 700-km-long unbroken segment between the ruptures

---

¶ A seismic gap is a part of an active plate boundary that has not generated any significant earthquakes for a long time, compared to its adjacent segments. The premise is that over long periods, displacement on any segment must be like what is experienced by the adjacent parts of the fault. So, the next earthquake must occur where there is a gap in time and space. By identifying seismic gaps, we can postulate on the region that might slip in the next earthquake.

of the great 1934 Bihar–Nepal and the 1905 Kangra earthquakes was identified as one such gap. Occupying the Garhwal and Kumaun regions of the central Himalayas, this segment was recognized as the 'central seismic gap'. The idea that an earthquake is imminent in the central Himalayas was reiterated by Roger Bilham, a research scientist at the University of Colorado, Boulder and his co-workers.[5] These researchers have used GPS[6]-based strain models to estimate the rate of motion between the two plates and the resulting stress build-up. In their view, the region has the potential to generate great earthquakes every 500 years. As the last earthquake occurred in 1505, the region is overdue for a great earthquake in their view.

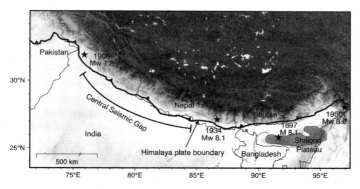

Figure 2.2: The plate boundary along the Himalayas showing the major earthquakes.

Was there any gap-filling earthquake that might have occurred here beyond the historically documented period? The 1803 Garhwal earthquake of magnitude ~7.6 was one significant event that needed a re-evaluation. Old temples in the region were witnesses to this earthquake, and by looking at the evidence such as the response of the great stone temples to ground shaking, we developed a tentative timeline of earthquakes that must have visited this region. Starting from the Katarmal Sun Temple of Almora, we traversed across the Garhwal and Kumaun regions. We studied how the temples in the Garhwal-Kumaun region sustained partial damage both from the 1803 earthquake and possibly much earlier earthquakes. The 1803 earthquake shook the capital city and brought down one of the cupolas of the twelfth-century Qutb Minar. Besides historical and archaeological inputs, the geological studies we conducted in the area also pointed to the fact that more damaging earthquakes of greater magnitudes than the 1803 event may have occurred in the central gap several hundred years ago.

Many earthquakes have rocked the Nepal and Bihar Himalayas as well as the north-eastern region of India. The great 1897 earthquake of Shillong, Meghalaya was not a Himalayan plate boundary earthquake but was in the outlying regions. This earthquake attained global attention due to its large size and impact and its occurrence at a time when modern seismographs had just come into wider use. It is not surprising that the earthquake opened new vistas in observational seismology and resulted in one of the finest monographs on any of the nineteenth-century earthquakes globally. A pioneer in earthquake studies, R.D. Oldham, working at the Geological Survey of India, prepared a classic report giving the details of destruction and ground failures and results of triangulation surveys from 1860.[7] His 1899 report also mentions about the extremely high ground acceleration.[**] During the 1897 earthquake the ground

---

[**] Peak Ground Acceleration: Shaking in an earthquake is commonly expressed as peak ground acceleration (PGA). Accelerations are

acceleration reportedly exceeded the Earth's gravitational acceleration, leading to unprecedented damage and disturbances to the landscape. Letters of Tom La Touche, a geologist working in the Geological Survey of India at that time, written to his wife, Nancy, reproduced by Roger Bilham give a vivid documentation of post-earthquake observations.[8] In his letter he gives a first-hand, day-by-day account of the effects of the earthquake and details of the damage and landscape changes that he witnessed. The 1897 earthquake was a lesson about how great earthquakes can destroy man-made structures and even transform the landscape. Ancient structures like bridges and temples that perished serve as archives of information about this earthquake. As we know that earthquakes do repeat, these archives offer the best tips to explore for any past earthquakes. The documented history of these structures serve as useful indicators to infer the timing of past earthquakes. Revisiting the 1897 earthquake by sifting through the historical, archaeological and geological evidence to get to its record of past earthquakes has been an exciting and challenging part of our investigations at any site of historical earthquakes.

The largest earthquake to have affected the Gangetic (Ganga) plains was the event of 15 January 1934 in the

---

typically measured in units of g, where g is the acceleration due to gravity on the surface of the Earth. Typical accelerations in earthquakes are between 0.05 and 1 g. 0.005 g would be barely felt, shaking over 0.05 g is unpleasant, and few buildings would survive an acceleration of more than 0.5 g. An acceleration of 1.0 g would throw you up in the air and slam you to the ground with twice the force of gravity alone. This rarely occurs in earthquakes and would cause catastrophic damage if it occurred for any length of time.

Bihar–Nepal border. The earliest of the twentieth-century great Himalayan earthquakes, this one gave a first glimpse of the unprecedented scale of ground deformation in a riverine landscape. The death toll in India and Nepal combined range from 7253 to as many as 25,000, as cited in a recent compilation.[9] This earthquake gave shape to the widely accepted model of earthquake genesis in the Himalayas—put forward by the seismologists Leonardo Seeber and his colleague John Armbruster.[10] In their model, all the great earthquakes nucleate beneath the Himalayas on the contact along which the Indian plate is sliding down beneath the Eurasian plate. The south-dipping the fault plane created in this process is where the stresses from the plate movements are accumulating. When a 1934-type earthquake occurs, the fault rupture would propagate southward and reach the surface or terminate midway. Because of their south-directed energy propagation, such earthquakes eventually affect the plains severely. They are more damaging because of the amplification by the alluvial soil found in the plains. The large liquefaction field produced by the 1934 earthquake provides evidence for such secondary effects. The descriptions and images in the form of damaged railway tracks, collapsed buildings and large sandblow craters formed by ejection of water are quite well-documented.

The north-east Himalayas are seismologically active because it is surrounded by many tectonic provinces—the Eastern Himalayan front to the north, the Mishmi Basin to the east, Indo-Myanmar to the south-east and the Shillong plateau in the south. Such active tectonism results in frequent earthquakes in the region. Some of them are very damaging, but many others are not very significant. In any case, north-east India is regarded as India's earthquake land.

The largest earthquake (magnitude 8.6) that independent India experienced was near Assam and it occurred in 1950 on Independence Day. Like the 1934 earthquake that shared its source region with Nepal, the 1950 event, generally referred to as the 'Assam earthquake', occurred close to the China–Tibet border, but its effects were largely felt in India. The then Prime Minister of India, Jawaharlal Nehru, in his broadcast to the nation over All India Radio, three weeks after the calamity, described the state of the mighty Brahmaputra River as '. . . blocked up for a while, and then broke through, they came down with rush and a roar, a high wall of water sweeping down and flooding large areas and washing away villages and fields and gardens . . . The remains of villages, animals, including cattle and elephants and large quantities of timber floated down these raging waters . . .'[11] Indeed, that is what the earthquake had done to the landscape, especially to the mighty Brahmaputra River. The ever-changing Brahmaputra River and the frequent floods that affect it have washed away the surface signatures created by the 1950 earthquake.

A Tsunami Surprise

In the late 1970s, at the University of Roorkee (now IIT Roorkee), the syllabus did cover earthquakes, but very little about tsunamis. Our teachers mentioned 'tsunamis' as large ocean waves caused by earthquakes along the coast of Japan. We were told that they had also occurred on the coasts of Alaska and Chile. 'What about India?' a student questioned. The teacher had a good laugh and told us not to worry. The only one that could be counted as an unusual wave was from the great Krakatoa volcanic explosion of 1883, he said. He went on to add that such explosions are far and few. However, he insisted that we need to know enough to write a short note on the topic. Yes, that was from the point of view of the examination. Sure enough, there was a five-mark question, and we were prepared to write a note. But we never considered its importance until the devastating tsunami struck the shores of South Asian countries on the day after Christmas in 2004.

On that lazy Sunday morning, we were at our home in Thiruvananthapuram, the capital city of Kerala, waking up late after the Christmas celebrations with visiting relatives. It was close to 8 a.m. when our telephones began to ring incessantly. Calls came from the coastal cities of Chennai, Kochi and many other distant places to inquire about an earthquake that had just occurred; they were not sure where. It was felt in his high-rise apartment in Kochi, one caller reported. We guessed that it could be a distant earthquake, and being a landfill area, the high-rises in Kochi usually feel the shaking, we explained to the caller. As we checked the United States Geological Survey (USGS) website,[12] we found that a great earthquake of magnitude 9.1 had occurred off the coast of Sumatra. The broadband station operated by the Centre for Earth Sciences at Thiruvananthapuram, about 300 km away, had recorded it too. A few minutes passed, and we responded with more details to the next round of calls: indeed, an earthquake had occurred in the ocean off Sumatra, but there was nothing to worry about in Kerala. We tried to contact our friends in Port Blair, but the telephone lines appeared dead. Nearly an hour passed, and the TV channels started reporting inundation along the Tamil Nadu Coast. More news came from Kanyakumari and the southern and central coastal strips of Kerala, mainly along the Kollam and Alappuzha districts. Images of death and destruction filled the

TV screens. Yes, it was a tsunami. Unprecedented not just in India, but also in the other affected countries: Indonesia, Thailand, Singapore and the Indian islands of Andaman and Nicobar in the east, Sri Lanka in the south, Maldives and as far as the shores of Africa in the west. They were killer waves.

The first wave, as a resident of Port Blair (South Andaman) described to us, was like a snake crawling gradually. He had felt the shaking, but his house withstood the earthquake. It seemed he just had to deal with the small tide. Sighing in relief, he started to wipe the floor and started to relax. But soon the 'crawling snake' transformed into a wall of water that closed in, knocked him down and drowned his home. Fortunately, he found a tree trunk to hang on to and survived. The waves had scoured the shores and deposited thick piles of sediments at many locations. There were several layers of them, marking the arrival of five or six surges which were separated in time.

In the temple city of Mamallapuram (Mahabalipuram), about 60 km away from Chennai, a large rock was exposed by scouring. The rocks, part of an ancient temple city, had inscriptions on them. Suspecting this to be the site of an old temple, the Archaeological Survey of India had started excavations here following the tsunami. As expected, they found the remains of an eighth-century temple. This was the place to look for the predecessors of any tsunami that must have visited this shore, we reckoned. And sure enough, within the basement ruins, we found a layer of sand enriched with deep marine organisms. Dated at about 1000 years old, this was the first evidence of a pre-2004 giant tsunami that had hit the Indian shores.

We were embarking on a new journey, searching for the footprints of ancient tsunamis not just along the

Indian shores but also in Southeast Asian countries—
Thailand, Indonesia, Sri Lanka and more. International
teams supported by the United Nations stepped in, led by
pioneers like Brian Atwater, Jeffrey Freymueller, George
Plafker, Kenji Satake and many others. We worked along
the shores of North America, Chile, Japan, Thailand and
many other countries to learn from the land-level changes
caused by great earthquakes and deposits left by tsunamis.
Atwater took CP through the remains of the dead trees in
the form of exposed stumps and fallen trunks, described as
ghost forests created by the 1964 Chile earthquake. Kusala
went to the Oregon Coast, where Atwater showed similar
stumps of cedar trees along the Columbia River; they
were killed by the 1700 CE Cascadia earthquake as their
roots got severed when the land was uplifted. Plafker led
our team to a similar archive of dead trees formed during
the 1960 Alaska earthquake, in trenches excavated near
Anchorage.

In the Andaman and Nicobar Islands, we found
evidence of both subsidence and uplift. At Indira Point,
the southernmost tip of the Indian subcontinent, not
very far from the source of Sumatra located to the south,
the lighthouse on the sandy beach surrounded by lush
vegetation was submerged under the sea. The ground sunk
by about 3 m, drowning the foundation of the lighthouse.
In North Andaman, the opposite motion had occurred—
the land was raised. In Diglipur, 700 km north of Great
Nicobar Island, the mangrove trees in the intertidal zone
were thrown up by about a metre. They were sitting on the
muddy platform with their roots exposed. The intertidal
bivalves clinging to the roots remained alive for a few days,
thanks to the high tide.

The Parkfield Experiment

Every time a new earthquake occurs, it throws up some surprises, requiring further refinement of our understanding of the phenomena. The most striking experience is from Parkfield, California, where a twenty-two-year regularity of moderate earthquakes (1857, 1881, 1901, 1922, 1934 and 1966) seemed ideal for a prediction experiment. As the USGS scientists explored, they figured out that all six moderate-size Parkfield earthquakes were 'characteristic'; all of them had ruptured the same part of the well-mapped fault. If there was such regularity, seismologists figured out that an earthquake of magnitude 6 or more was due before 1993.[13] While in waiting, a smaller one of less than magnitude 5 occurred on 20 October 1992. Regarded as the potential foreshock of an imminent earthquake, an alert was issued. At that time, Evelyn Roeloffs, in charge of monitoring the groundwater fluctuations, was in South Carolina as the doctoral thesis examiner for Kusala's defence, scheduled for 21 October. Past midnight, Evelyn received a call, and she had to leave on the next available flight. The defence had to be rescheduled. The earthquake that was predicted also went off schedule. It came sixteen years later, on 28 September 2004, without giving any signals of its arrival. The Parkfield story is a compelling example of how the presence or absence of aftershocks gives no definite clues about an impending earthquake, as we discussed earlier.

* * *

Liquefaction and Sandblows

Liquefaction is the process by which the strength and stiffness of a soil is lost when loosely packed, water-logged sediments at or near the ground surface lose their strength in response to strong ground shaking. Liquefaction occurring beneath buildings and other structures can cause major damage during earthquakes. Liquefaction may also lead to the formation of sandblows, also known as sand boils or sand volcanoes which are formed by the ejection of sand on to a surface from a central point. The ejected sand builds up as a cone and a crater is commonly formed. The ejection of sand forms an intrusive dike, which are used by earthquake geologists as a sign of earthquake induced liquefaction. Any organic remains like twigs or charcoal are used to obtain the age of the liquefaction event.

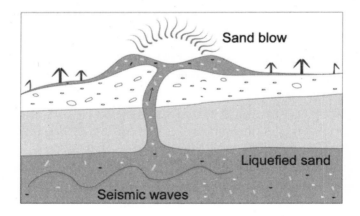

Figure 2.3: Cross-section of a sand blow formed during earthquake.

Chapter 3

Theatre of Earth Where the Show Never Stops

It takes an earthquake to remind us that we walk on the crust of an unfinished planet.
        —*Charles Kuralt, CBS Television Host*

Students of geology in the 1950s would have marvelled at the peaks of Mt Everest and wondered what forces could have resulted in their elevation. The rocks of Mt Everest, carrying fossil-bearing marine limestones that are 458–85 million years old, would only have added to their bewilderment. A conservative student would be tempted to rely on 'catastrophism' that credits the features seen on the surface of Earth, such as mountains, to catastrophes. This idea suggests that certain geological conditions that existed in the past do not exist today. However, a non-conservative student might draw upon theories propounded by James Hutton[1] and Charles Lyell.[2] She may use uniformitarianism* and the famous maxim 'the present

---

* Geologists James Hutton and Charles Lyell developed the theory of uniformitarianism. The basis of this theory is that geological events

is the key to the past' and argue that Mt Everest is part of a landscape that formed over a long period through gradual processes. Through the lens of uniformitarianism, modern-day geologic events, some as sudden as an earthquake, and others as slow as erosion, are a window into past events. Lyell had argued that sudden and immense catastrophes did not create mountain chains, but they grew almost imperceptibly over geological time[†] through successive movements and uplifts. It is mind-boggling to count the number of uplift events that have taken the fossiliferous limestones on the seabed to an elevation of about 8 km!

Charles Darwin witnessed one such event—the great 1835 Concepción (Chile) earthquake—while on the HMS *Beagle*,[3] the British naval vessel which was on a voyage to South America and around the world (1831–36). He witnessed the event while at the shore of Valdivia, a city in central Chile, 320 kilometres south of Concepción. Meanwhile, at the nearby island of Santa María, the HMS *Beagle*'s Captain Robert FitzRoy[4] noticed putrid mussel shells clinging to the rocks, three metres above the high-tide level. It looked as if an instant event had lifted these

---

always occur in uniform ways and present events, such as an earthquake act as windows to the past events. In other words, we learn about the past of the earth looking at its present.

[†] Geologic time scale represents a 'calendar' of events that happened on the Earth since its formation about 4.6 billion years ago. Segments of time which run into millions of years are represented by rock layers. Presence of fossils often helps to identify the onset and termination of time intervals. Major geologic events such as the appearance (or the disappearance) of significant species (like the extinction of the dinosaurs about 65 million years ago) mark the boundaries of these segments.

creatures out of their habitat and killed them on the site. The earthquake that Darwin witnessed was a snapshot in time and one among the numerous events that have shaped the Earth.

Interestingly, Darwin had made his deductions about land uplift even before Captain FitzRoy found the mussels lifted out of their habitats. At Chiloé, an island off the coast of Chile, Darwin had noticed a thick bed of oyster shells sitting at more than 100 metres above the tide level. Similarly, he found petrified remains of a forest, with the trees fossilized in their upright position, at an elevation of more than 2100 metres above sea level in the Andes of Argentina. As noted in his diary,[5] he explained that the trees initially grew above sea level but died as they were plunged below sea level for a short period of time and raised again afterwards. Darwin could not explain how this type of vertical movement took place. Still, as he spent the next few weeks in the region, travelling inland to the mountains, it was clear that the uplift of coastal tracts did not occur at random. Remains of marine shells found far inland and at elevated locations suggested successive shifts and uplifts of the coast in the recent geological past. By looking at this earthquake-prone country and its emerging landscape, Darwin was convinced that Charles Lyell was right about the origin of mountains through successive movements and uplifts. Darwin could see that the 1835 uplift was just one event, a moment in the ongoing shaping of the Earth.

Earth in Turmoil, a popular book on earthquakes by Kerry Sieh and Simon LeVay, considers such an event as 'a moment in the creation of the world'.[6] One such moment is the 23 October 1983 Central Idaho earthquake (M_w 6.9) which is brought to life through a captivating eyewitness account. Lawana Knox, who witnessed the earthquake, was on an elk-hunting trail on that crisp autumn morning.

Sitting on a dry stream bed, she was aiming at her target which was grazing on the hillside. Suddenly, she became aware of an unusual rumbling and trembling of the ground. Before her eyes, the ground tore apart and she was placed on the up-thrown side of the tear. The tear that elevated the land and Knox is what the geologists would describe as a normal-fault. In that fortuitous moment, the elk slipped down from her line of sight and its life was saved by the earthquake! The tear that vertically moved Knox and her target was not small. The Lost River fault, as it is known, extends for about 35 km. The uplift of ground measured 3 m at some locations along this fault. Following the idea that the present can tell us about the past, earthquake geologists turn to such features to find evidence for past earthquakes. They liken their work to that of a detective at the scene of a crime, and they are generally right in their deductions.

The Orphan Tsunami of 1700: Japanese Clues to a Parent Earthquake in North America, a book by Brian Atwater of the US Geological Survey and Japanese co-authors Kenji Satake and Satoko Musumi-Rokkaku, reads almost like a detective story.[7] The authors used the roots of red cedar trees on the banks of the Columbia River to make their case. During his field surveys, Atwater noticed several dead trees on the land. The low tide exposed decaying roots of large trees jutting out of water. Atwater reasoned this to be the effect of land level changes due to the earthquake that caused both uplift and subsidence. He reasoned that where the land was uplifted, the roots were severed and the trees died. Where the land subsided, the red cedar trees died as they could not survive in water. There were also trees whose roots were partly severed, which started to regrow. By using the exact age of the strained tree ring, the scientists estimated that the trees died during the spring of 1700 CE. Atwater's findings opened a new area of investigation in tsunami geology research. Evidence from modern-day earthquakes in Alaska, Chile and Indonesia has confirmed Atwater's hypothesis.

What Charles Darwin and Lawana Knox witnessed and what Brian Atwater and his co-workers dug up from geological archives are only a few snapshots of the earth's dynamism. Mountains must have grown indiscernibly over time, just as Charles Lyell conceived, but could they be rising due to millions of earthquakes? If not, why are major mountain chains like the Alps, Atlas, Andes and the Himalayas seismically active, and why are some, like the Andes and Cascadia, are also lined up with active volcanoes behind them? We need more than earthquakes to answer these questions and to explain the presence of marine fossils atop Mt Everest. This leads us to the next question—why do earthquakes occur, and why do they have an organized pattern of global distribution? The answer lies in plate tectonics, a theory that changed the outlook of geosciences in the 1960s.

Solving the Jigsaw Puzzle: A Revolution Begins

The Earth's surface is the biggest jigsaw puzzle ever designed. The first person to disassemble the pieces of this grand puzzle and join them with some scientific reasoning was Alfred Wegener (1880–1930), the German meteorologist and explorer. It wouldn't be correct to say that what Wegener formulated was entirely new. Between 1889 and 1909, the Italian violinist and geologist Roberto Mantovani published a theory that argued that the continents were fragmented due to thermal expansion after making an analogy with cracks in the Earth's surface that had been formed during volcanic eruptions. In his paper of 1909, Mantovani presented a map of the Pacific, with dotted lines drawn between pairs of geographic points that were in contact once, but were separated by the Pacific basin. When Wegener first presented his theory—in lectures delivered in 1912 and published in full in 1915 in his most important work, *Die Entstehung der Kontinente und Ozeane* (The Origin of Continents and Oceans)—he had relied on Mantovani's maps to show the shape of the former continents.

Wegener thought of this idea when he noticed how the distinct large landmasses of the Earth almost fit together like a jigsaw puzzle. He noticed that many present continents would fit well if the intervening oceans vanished. Across continents, he saw an apparent continuity in the shape of some mountain ranges, the composition of rocks and other geological structures. The existence of identical species of plants and animals on different continents was key biological evidence. For example, fossils of plants and animals of similar age and species were found on the shores of the western coast of Africa and the eastern coast of Brazil. The most compelling among the transoceanic evidence was the remains of *Mesosaurus*, a freshwater crocodile-like reptile that lived during the early Permian Period (between 286 and 258 million years ago). It would have been physiologically impossible for *Mesosaurus* to swim across the Atlantic Ocean, and hence it was concluded that these continental blocks must have been together. Based on all the evidence he collected, Wegener joined the fragmented continents and recreated their parent landmass and is known as 'Pangea' meaning, all-land.

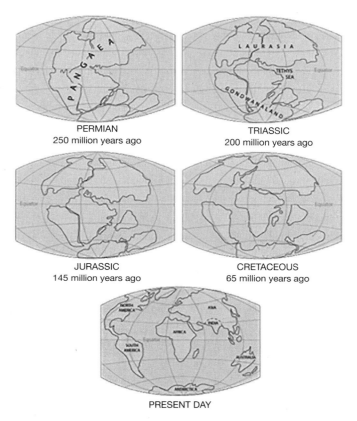

Figure 3.1: Wegener's reconstruction of continental drift.

The climate records looked even more curious, which Wegener used as support for his hypothesis. It is well-known that as a continent moves towards the equator, its climate becomes warmer, and as it moves towards the poles, it gets cooler. If a continent in a specific climatic zone drifts away from its earlier location and joins another from a different zone, the amalgamated land would showcase fossils from both continents. Fossils of 300-million-year-old tropical plants were found on Spitsbergen, an island in the Arctic Ocean. Similarly, tropical fossils of the Carboniferous Period (280 million years ago) were found in the Mediterranean, and glacial rocks of the same age were found in India—both currently occupying similar latitudes. For the glacial rocks to form and for India to be cooler, it had to be several degrees south of its current position.

Based on the observation that landmasses could be backtracked as Pangea, Wegener proposed that continents must have moved several thousands of kilometres before they reached their present positions. That idea led to the theory of continental drift. It was an attractive idea that solved the jigsaw puzzle, but several questions were not answered. What was the driving mechanism behind the drift? How could large continental masses plough their way for thousands of kilometres? And how were the oceans created? Wegener had suggested that the continents had drifted apart, but he could not explain what drove this movement. His idea was almost forgotten, and the concept of continental drift resurfaced only decades later. Geological science was about to undergo a paradigm shift. Scientific tools employed during World War II brought scientists closer to finding the mechanism for continental drift. Seismometers installed as part of the World-Wide Standardized Seismographic Network (WWSSN)[8] in 1965 allowed improved detection of earthquake locations. Very soon it was evident that the global earthquake distribution was not random, but they had some spatial associations.

Magnetic surveys to locate submarines, another post-World War initiative, led to some startling discoveries. The surveys recorded magnetic field variations in successive bands of rocks on the ocean floor. While some rocks were aligned with the current magnetic field, some others showed opposite polarity. This pattern was important evidence for seafloor spreading, a concept that was to become central to the theory of plate tectonics. Harry H. Hess, an American geophysicist used this new evidence to propose the theory of 'seafloor spreading'. In *The History of Ocean Basins*[9] of 1962, he proposed the seafloor spreading hypothesis and explained how the new oceanic crust formed along the mid-ocean ridges moves laterally and eventually dives deep into the mantle at the trenches. He explained how the magma cools and hardens along the ridges on the ocean floor and how the outer shells of the earth or the plates move sideways as if on a conveyor belt. This movement causes the continents to drift. The idea of sea floor spreading proved that Wegner was right in his argument about drifting continents, a theory that fell short of a sustainable driving mechanism. Anchored on a deeper understanding of the internal structure of the Earth and the global earthquake data, the theory of plate tectonics provided the driving mechanism. Wegener died in November 1930 during an Arctic expedition before he could celebrate the scientific validation of his theory. But it laid the foundations for a revolution in Earth science that was to begin by the mid-1960s.

Plate Tectonics Explains It All

Recognizing the forces enabling the movement of continents had been the missing ingredient in Wegener's theory that had led to its rejection. However, revisiting the idea of continental drift after the emergence of sea floor spreading led to a more daring proposition—the theory of plate tectonics. By the mid-1960, multiple groups were using the idea of seafloor spreading and the data from the WWSSN to understand the internal structure of the earth and its manifestations on the surface of the earth. Jason Morgan of Princeton University was the first to make a formal presentation on the idea of plate tectonics. Morgan used ocean floor data to argue that the pattern of fracture zones are the result of relative movement of plates. His talk at the April 1967 meeting of the American Geophysical Union (AGU) in Washington included all the key theoretical ideas of plate tectonics. Although Morgan took the lead in presenting the idea of plate tectonics, his paper was published only a year later, in March 1968.[10] In the meantime, two other scientists— Dan McKenzie and Bob Parker—independently wrote a joint paper for *Nature* in 1967,[11] presenting fresh ideas about plate tectonics. Their research findings showed that the Earth was far more dynamic than previously thought. Their idea that the Earth's mantle has two layers which are in constant motion provided the basic mechanism for the movement of tectonic plates. A year later, Bryan L. Isacks, Jack Oliver and Lynn R. Sykes,[12] geophysicists at the Lamont-Doherty Earth Observatory at Columbia University presented the most convincing argument based on the study of global seismicity. Using the WWSSN data they showed that the distribution of earthquakes was confined to narrow and continuous belts that bound large continental areas. The data also allowed inferences about the mechanism of faulting along these belts. The mid-oceanic ridges where magma is coming out were marked by shallow (around 10-15 km deep) earthquakes. Their mechanism showed extension, consistent with the bulging of magma chamber beneath the crust. On the contrary, trenches were dominated by compressional tectonics, consistent with the collision of two plates. Earthquakes were shallow as well as a few hundred kilometres deep, demonstrating the geometry of the sinking lithosphere. Further, the spatial distribution of earthquakes grossly defined the configuration of the down-going slabs. The 1968 paper by Isacks and Oliver provided the framework for plate tectonics with a strong scientific basis. In the words of Larry Brown, a former student of Jack Oliver, that paper 'was the Bible for understanding seismology'.[13]

As Earth-science students of the mid-1970s, we also read that 'Bible', along with many gospels that made us passionate about plate tectonics. In our laboratories, we would use cuttings from old world maps to solve the jigsaw puzzle. Geophysics professors returning from Western universities after postdoctoral research would talk excitedly about the revolution in the offing. They would draw pictures to demonstrate the geometries of sea-floor spreading, and explain how the data from post-World War II ocean expeditions generated these maps. Mountain ranges running for more than 16,000 km in the Atlantic, now known as the Mid-Atlantic Ridge, were the most outstanding features of this newly discovered underwater topography. There were similar features in other oceans too, nearly 80,000 km of them winding around continents.

The spectacular topographic features of the ocean floor and the association of earthquakes with such distinctive geographic regions were becoming more evident with the new data that was emerging. Seismological evidence not only defined the distinctive spatial pattern of global earthquake distribution, but it also helped image the Earth's interior structure. The distribution of the Earth's internal heat, its layered structure and the organization of its fragmented outer shells or plates that could glide over the partially molten underlying layer, were the essential elements of this new theory. The theory of plate tectonics was able to reconstruct the position of the continents in the past and predict their future positions in timescales of millions of years. Scientists could now explain most (if not all) features on Earth—continents, ocean basins, mountain ranges, deep-sea trenches, earthquakes, volcanoes and more. They could also explain how organisms that had previously lived together on older and amalgamated continental masses were now separated and had evolved independently.

With time, several path-breaking ideas strengthened the foundations of the plate tectonic theory. One such breakthrough was the discovery of reversals in the magnetic field of the earth with their imprints on the ocean floor. The curious nature of the Earth's magnetic field that occasionally reverts its polarity had been noticed even before the theory of plate tectonics was propounded. It was known from studies of land-based volcanic rocks that Earth's magnetic polarity had reversed numerous times in the geological past. But the data from land was scattered. Oceanographic expeditions in the 1950s mapped the magnetic character of the basaltic sea floor for long distances without break. The maps showed basaltic rocks on both sides of the mid-ocean ridge, with ages increasing away from their crest. As geologists studied their magnetic polarity, they discovered that in many of these rocks, iron minerals were aligned towards the south magnetic pole, not to the north. The bands of basalts with different polarities were marked as black and white patches, like that of a zebra, and were called magnetic stripes.

Although magnetic stripes were mapped in the 1950s, they remained unexplained until two British geoscientists, Frederick John Vine and Drummond Hoyle Matthews of Cambridge University, shed light on their intriguing pattern of polarity reversal. In a paper published in the journal *Nature*,[14] they proposed the 'Vine-Matthews-Morley hypothesis', adding Lawrence Morley, a Canadian geophysicist, who had independently come up with the same idea. Their idea was that as new oceanic crust forms through the solidification of magma, the rocks acquire a magnetization consistent with the magnetic field prevailing at that time. Thus, when the magnetic field of the earth points towards the north magnetic pole, as it does today, the rocks show 'normal' polarity. When the field points towards the south magnetic pole, which is the opposite of its present configuration, the field and the rocks would show 'reversed' polarity. It follows that rocks of the same age would show the same polarity. As the rock samples can be analysed for their ages and polarity, the magnetic stripes on the ocean floor is akin to a tape recorder with the history of reversals. Further, the age of the basalt and their distance from the crest of the ridge allowed the geologists to estimate the rate of spreading. The data from the ocean floor shows that the Earth's magnetic field has reversed itself many times in the past.

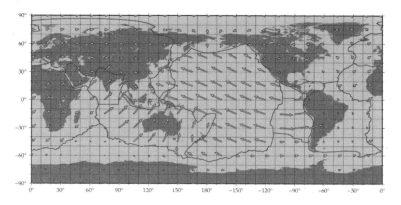

Figure 3.2: Major tectonic plates and the plate motion trajectories.

With the mapping of the seafloor and the acceptance of the theory of seafloor spreading, ridges were recognized as one type of plate boundary. They were designated as the constructive or the divergent boundary where plates diverge as new material is being generated. The mid-Atlantic ridge that began forming about 200 million years ago and resulted in today's Atlantic Ocean is a good example of a divergent boundary. Where deep-sea trench systems border the continents, as in the Pacific Ocean, the plates converge and the ocean floor dives downwards, under-thrusting the continents and ultimately joining the Earth's mantle. The crust is lost along these boundaries. Thus, they are known as convergent or destructive boundaries, such as the Aleutian convergence boundary between the North American Plate and the Pacific Plate. Both these types of boundaries are associated with earthquakes and volcanism, as explained by plate tectonics.

While the seafloor spreading theory explained the formation of oceans and helped to estimate the rate of movement of plates, it could not explain why there were the active volcanoes on the ocean floors. Interestingly, they were located many thousands of kilometres away from the ridges, which were conduits of magma. In 1963, John Tuzo Wilson, a Canadian geophysicist, proposed that plates might move over fixed locations called 'hotspots', which are conduits of magma connected with the mantle. He proposed that plates might move over fixed 'hotspots' where magma rises from the Earth's mantle, forming volcanic island chains like Hawaii.[15] Tuzo Wilson is also credited with the discovery of a third type of plate boundary—the conservative boundary or transform faults—where two plate slide sideways past each other without creating or destroying any oceanic crust.[16] The San Andreas Fault is an example of a continental transform fault that extends roughly 1200 km through California, USA. Global models of plate motions computed using geological data, mostly the age-distance relationship of magnetic rocks, were averaged over a few millions of years. The emergence of space geodetic techniques, especially GPS, made it possible to estimate the angular velocity of plates. NUVEL-1, published by Charles DeMets and his co-workers in 1990,[17] is a basic model that explains global plate motions. Modern-day GPS models provide estimates of movements across fault zones, allowing seismologists to estimate the rate of movement and infer the build-up of strain.

Earthquakes as proof of plate tectonics

Observational and theoretical research had made several significant advances in Japan, North America and Europe by the 1930s. The strongest evidence for the operation of plate tectonics came from the study of earthquakes. In their classic treatise written in 1965, *Seismicity of the Earth, and Associated Phenomena*,[18] Beno Gutenberg and Charles Richter documented several observations about the geographic distribution of earthquakes that helped establish the plate-tectonic theory. They observed that most large earthquakes occur in narrow belts that outline a set of stable blocks. They also suggested that nearly all intermediate and deep earthquakes are associated with planar zones that dip beneath volcanic island arcs, and that seismicity in the ocean basins is concentrated near the crest of the oceanic ridges and rises. The strongest evidence that reiterated the theory of plate tectonics came from the WWSSN that lead to an improved map of global earthquakes.

The 1964 earthquake (M_w 9.2) in south-central Alaska was a milestone in earthquake research. This was the first great earthquake to have occurred since the inception of the WWSSN. Data from about seventy stations allowed scientists to study its origin. This was also one of the earliest earthquakes that allowed seismologists to study the spectacular land-level changes they caused. About 300 km south-west of the earthquake, the land near Kodiak was permanently raised by 9 m. South-east of Anchorage, some areas dropped as much as 2.4 m. The accompanying tsunami occurred due to the sinking of the oceanic Pacific plate under the continental North American plate, displacing a large water column.

With more data from the WWSSN, seismologists could study the patterns of global earthquakes with greater clarity. In 1969, Muawia Barazangi and James Dorman published a picture of the worldwide distribution of 29,553 earthquakes from January 1961 to December 1967.[19] The correspondence of the earthquake epicentres with the plate boundaries in their map was unambiguous. The science of seismology made significant advances in the later years. Locating earthquakes with precision, modelling their sources, mapping the prominent fault zones and imaging the interior structure of the Earth became possible. Today, the Global Seismographic Network (GSN), coordinated by Incorporated Research Institutions for Seismology (IRIS), the United States Geological Survey (USGS) and many other agencies around the world, contributes to the global studies of earthquakes. We know much more about the seismicity on Earth thanks to the efforts of various research organizations and universities.

Major tectonic boundaries on an active planet

Tectonically, the most happening places on Earth are the plate boundaries. Every textbook on global tectonics starts with a discussion on the features that explain the major outcome of plate motions—earthquakes, volcanoes and mountain building. There are different types of plate boundaries, divergent (conservative), convergent (destructive) and conservative (transform). New crust is being generated along the divergent boundaries. The sideways push from the solidified magma causes the plate to move apart along the chain of submarine volcanic mounts known as the mid-oceanic ridges, rising 2–3 km on the ocean floor. The mid-Atlantic ridge, for example, was formed when two pairs of tectonic plates were spread apart (North America/Eurasia in the north; South America/Africa in the south). Along the convergent boundaries, one of the plates dives down and the crust is destroyed. If the plates that converge are part of continental blocks (thicker and less dense), as is the case for the Indian and the Eurasian plates, the collision will result in a mountain range, like the Himalayas. If one of the plates is oceanic and hence denser than the continental plate it is abutting against, the denser plate is forced to plunge deep underneath. The result is subduction, as happened for instance when the oceanic part of the Indian plate plunged beneath the Eurasian plate along the Andaman—Sumatra plate boundary. In addition to great earthquakes and tsunamis (as witnessed in 2004), these plate boundaries are also prone to volcanic activity (the 1883 eruption of Krakatoa, the Indonesian volcano is an example). Along the conservative boundaries the plate slide past each other, with no creation and no destruction. Along this plate boundary faults connect oceanic ridges or ocean trenches and allow plates to slide past each other. With the orientation of transform faults generally parallel to the plate motions, their offsets provide estimate of the rate of plate motions.

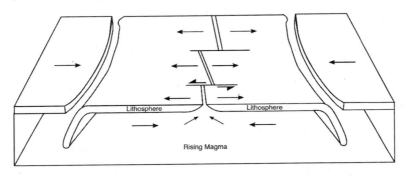

Figure 3.3: An overview of the tectonic processes along the plate boundaries.

The pattern of world seismicity observed before the plate tectonic revolution was suggestive of a pattern which became clearer once the plate boundaries were identified. Narrow bands of seismicity overlap with the oceanic ridges and the transform faults. Broad zones of earthquakes mark the collision boundaries, continental (India–Eurasia along the Himalayas) or oceanic (Nazca–South America plates along the Chile subduction zone). The deeper earthquakes (>600 km) are restricted to the subduction zones where the plate is pushed under the overriding plate. Finally, there is the unmistakable presence of the volcanoes along the trenches.

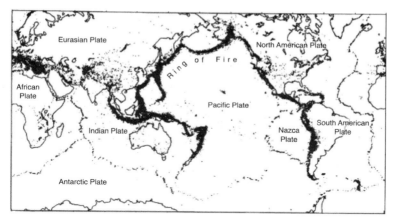

Figure 3.4: Worldwide distribution of large magnitude earthquakes (magnitude greater than 4): 1961–67 after Muawia Barazangi and James Dorman, 1967.

The ring of fire: Live kiln of the plate tectonic engine

The ring of fire, or the circum-Pacific belt, is perhaps the most spectacular expression of plate tectonic activity on the Earth. The ring, not exactly circular, is about 40,000 km long, and runs along the boundaries between the Pacific, Juan de Fuca, Cocos, Indian–Australian, Nazca, North American and Philippine plates. Seventy-five per cent of Earth's volcanoes (approximately 1500) and 90 per cent of its earthquakes occur along the ring of fire. The spatial correspondence of the ring with the arcuate chain of active volcanoes is not accidental. These are factories that recycle magma. The oceanic crust that sinks deep into the Earth re-emerges through these edifices millions of years later. History is replete with notorious volcanic eruptions along the ring of fire; the 79 CE eruption of Mount

Vesuvius and the 1883 eruption of Krakatoa are some of the most devastating among them. The Yellowstone super-volcano, part of the ring of fire, erupted about 6,40,000 years ago. It was no ordinary show. The large area that erupted collapsed upon itself, creating a sunken giant crater or caldera of about 3900 sq. km. Walking around Yellowstone National Park, one might find it difficult to locate the volcano because it occupies the entire park. The bubbling geysers and hot springs that attract visitors are indications of the churning activity below the surface.

On 10 April 1815, the Indonesian island of Sumbawa became the scene of a massive volcanic eruption. Known as the Mount Tambora event, it is the worst in modern history. Ejecting about 100 megatons of sulphur aerosols into the stratosphere, its impact was felt all over the globe. A long winter in the west and an erratic monsoon in Southeast Asia that caused a famine in India were the major fallout of this eruption. The Barren Island in the Andaman Sea, the only volcano in India, erupted on 24 August 2005.[20] The mild explosion on this small volcanic island was a reminder that it was alive and that the story was not over yet.

Is there more room for the unexpected? In nature, they say, we must count the last 1 per cent of the unknown. On 14 January 2022, the underwater volcano Hunga Tonga-Hunga Ha'apai off Tonga demonstrated that the Earth could shock its inhabitants with surprises. Geographically relegated to a distant corner of the southern Pacific Ocean, the Polynesian island nation of Tonga, an archipelago of more than a hundred tiny islands, witnessed a colossal volcanic eruption. The explosive activity early in the morning of 15 January was the most violent in the last thirty years of the global record of volcanism. The eruption generated a 20 km high mushroom cloud of smoke and ash in the near field and sent shockwaves halfway around the planet, triggering an oil leak near Peru and raising concerns of a tsunami across the Pacific. The low-lying unpopulated islands nearby were indeed inundated by 4–5 m high waves in the aftermath of the initial event. The story of Tonga tells us that we are indeed walking on a planet in the making. It is indeed unfinished work.

* * *

Faults

A fault is a zone of fracture between two blocks of rocks that allows movement of blocks with respect to each other. The angle of the fault plane with respect to the surface is the dip; the direction in which the block is slipping is the strike.

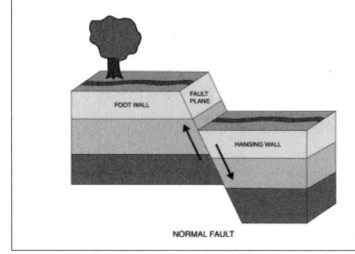

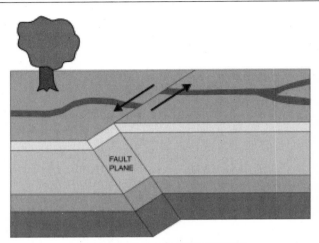

STRIKE-SLIP FAULT (LEFT LATERAL)

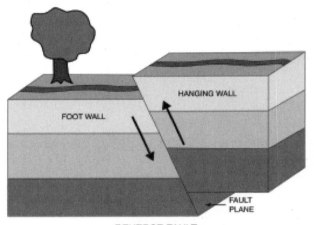

REVERSE FAULT

Figure 3.5: Sketches showing different types of faults.
On the previous page: *normal fault is a dip-slip fault in which the block above the fault plane moves downward.* Top: *strike-slip fault, where the two blocks on either side of the fault plane slide past one another.* Bottom: *reverse or thrust fault is a dip-slip fault in which the upper block, above the fault plane, moves up over the lower block.*

Faults that move along the direction of the dip plane are called dip-slip faults. In a normal fault, the block above the fault plane (hanging wall) moves downward relative to the block below it (footwall). Normal faulting occurs in response to extensional stresses, as observed along oceanic ridge systems or continental rift systems (For e.g., East African rift). Faults in which blocks move along a horizontal plane are known as strike-slip faults. A reverse (thrust) fault is one in which the hanging wall moves up relative to the foot wall (and thus is the opposite of a normal fault). Thrust faults occur in response compression, as it happens along the continental collision zones (e.g., Himalayan mountains) or along regions where one plate is being subducted (e.g., Sumatra trench). Some thrust faults are not visible on the surface and they are called blind thrusts. As there are no surface expressions, blind-thrust earthquakes can occur at unexpected locations and they can be very destructive. The 2001 Bhuj earthquake is considered a blind-thrust earthquake.

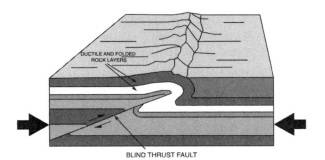

Figure 3.6: A blind-thrust fault that has terminated below the surface forming a fold. It creates a mount-like feature on the surface, leaving no surface expression of ground break.

Folds

Folding is often the result of increased horizontal stress or compression. In geology, a fold represents an undulation in the layers of rocks of the Earth's crust. It is somewhat like applying pressure on a stack of pancakes (imagine that each pancake is a layer of rock). Folding occurs in all kinds of rocks, but they are more spectacular in layered sedimentary rocks. Sediment deposited by the action of water or wind occur as horizontal beds and subsequently form layered sedimentary rocks. However, due to the forces acting on the Earth, rocks rarely retain their horizontal layering. When compressive stresses act on the rocks they get compacted. As the horizontal rock layers bend vertically, they get warped or folded. Folds vary widely in size—several to even hundreds of kilometres across, or just a few centimetres or less.

As tectonic plates collide along compressing boundaries, rocks and debris are warped and folded into rocky outcrops, hills, mountains or entire mountain ranges. The rugged, soaring heights of the Himalayas, Andes and Alps are all active fold mountains. As tectonic forces originating from plate motions continue to push the rocks, folds continue to grow and propagate forward. When the slip along a propagating thrust fault is reduced to zero, the fault terminates by converting the shortening as folding. Over an extended period of time they form a special class of folds, known as fault-propagation folds.

The collided mountain ranges of the Himalayas display some of the best examples fault-propagation folds.

FAULT-PROPAGATION FOLD

Figure 3.7: A fault-propagation fold showing how the thrust fault has terminated, leading to the formation of a fold.

Chapter 4

Ascent of Earthquake Science

Earthquakes travelling through the interior of the globe are like so many messengers sent out to explore a new land. The messages are constantly coming, and seismologists are fast learning to read them.
—Reginald Aldworth Daly

The history of seismology has been traced to some 4000 years ago when humans started to witness the phenomena of earthquakes and volcanoes. As an observant species, humans have been aware of earthquakes since their existence; they are alluded to in early religious scriptures and folklore in the proto-historic cultures extending from Iran to India. But for most of human history, their cause was not understood. The most common explanation for earthquakes in the early cultures was the same as that of all other natural disasters—divine wrath. Two premodern cultures, the Chinese and the Greek, offered natural explanations. Aristotle (circa 330 BCE) was one of the first to attempt an explanation for earthquakes based on natural phenomena when he postulated that winds from within the Earth caused the occasional shaking. The Chinese put forth similar ideas about earthquakes around the same time, and Zhang Heng[1] developed the technology for the first seismoscope in 132 CE. Empirical observations of the effects of earthquakes were rare until 1750, when a series of five strong earthquakes uncharacteristically rocked England. In a similar incident on 1 November 1755, when many people were in the churches praying on All Saints Day, a cataclysmic shock and tsunami killed an estimated 70,000 people, levelling the city of Lisbon, Portugal. This devastating temblor and the tsunami disrupted the Portuguese empire and challenged the European Enlightenment-era optimism. Some Enlightenment philosophers observed that if people had taken appropriate action after the initial temblor, many lives could have been saved from the consequent tsunami—maybe the first attempt to conceptualize what is now known as 'vulnerability'. Perhaps this event marks the beginning of the modern era of seismology, as it also prompted scientific studies on the frequency and locations of earthquakes.

Robert Mallet, an Irish engineer, who was attracted to the propositions by Charles Lyell—that scientific laws governed geological actions—made significant contributions to the science of seismology. The first catalogue of earthquakes, credited to several individuals, was published in 1840. This was followed by the design of the first mechanical seismometer in 1841. Thus, seismology as a science was born. Mallet's book,[2] based on papers he read to the Royal Irish Academy between 1842 and 1846, was another milestone. Mallet also coined the terms seismology, epicentre, seismic focus, isoseismals and angle of emergence. His two-volume work, *Great Neapolitan Earthquake of 1857: The First Principles of Seismology* on the 1857 Naples (Italy) earthquake,[3] the first post-earthquake field investigation report, presented observations buttressed by photographs at a time when field photography was practically non-existent. According to him, earthquakes were caused 'either by the sudden flexure and constraint of the elastic materials forming a portion of the Earth's crust or by their giving way and becoming fractures'.

In India, Thomas Oldham (1816–78), the first superintendent of the Geological Survey of India (GSI), made seminal contributions in seismology inspired by Mallet's monograph. He used Mallet's ideas to study the Cachar (northeast India) earthquake of 1869. The great 1897 Shillong earthquake that rocked north-east India, one of the largest to be recorded by instruments, enabled the significant discovery of the Earth's interior. Richard Dixon Oldham followed the 1897 earthquake and used the seismic records located between 6900 and 7800 km from the epicentre to prove the existence of three phases of seismic waves. He identified them as compressional (P) and shear (S) traversing the body of the Earth and the third one that causes surface undulations travelling around the world (surface waves). These findings led to the discovery of the Earth's internal structure and the identification of its core.

At the same time, an early leap in earthquake science took place in Japan when it welcomed foreign experts as a part of its open-door policy, known in history as the Meiji Restoration. This move allowed a young geologist and mining engineer, John Milne, to join the College of Technology in Tokyo. His tenure coincided with an earthquake in 1880, which motivated him to develop the first seismic recorder along with James Ewing, an American professor at Tokyo University. The 1891 earthquake of magnitude ~8.0, located somewhere between Tokyo and Osaka, was a turning point in seismology that energized Milne's students to map the causative fault rupture and monitor the aftershocks. One of them, Fusakichi Omori, later formulated the celebrated theory that the rate of aftershocks decreases quickly with time; the theory was named Omori's law. By the latter part of the nineteenth century, scientific research on earthquakes was firmly in place in Japan. Driven by passion, Omori travelled from Tokyo to India, to study the 4 April 1905 earthquake in Kangra, Himachal Pradesh. Using the seismic recorders he had designed, he located and monitored the smaller shocks that followed the main quake. Then he moved to Formosa, Taiwan, to monitor an earthquake that occurred on 17 March 1906, and a month later, he hopped on to a boat to San Francisco, the location of the 18 April 1906 earthquake of magnitude 7.9.

The 1906 San Francisco Earthquake Led to a Path-Breaking Theory

Three Fearful Days,[4] edited by Malcolm Barker, tells moving stories of the 1906 San Francisco (California) earthquake that shook people out of their slumber. California is home to Hollywood and a lot of earthquakes. The people here know their city is built on the ~1200 km long San Andreas fault system, one of Earth's largest linear fault lines. Nearly six decades after the earthquake, the theory of plate tectonics would explain that the great earthquake occurred on the San Andreas fault, a transform (strike-slip) boundary between the northern Pacific and the North American plates.

Figure 4.1: Offset along the San Andreas fault.

Over much of its length, the presence of the San Andreas fault is evident from the air through its linear arrangement of lakes, bays and valleys. On the ground, however, the features are more subtle, but expressed by distinctive landforms, including long, straight escarpments, narrow ridges and many stream channels that characteristically jog sharply to the right as they cross the fault. The measured offset of streams across the sliding blocks, indicating the movement along the fault, was estimated as 4–6 cm per year since the early twentieth century. Parts of the fault line moved as much as 6.4 m during the 1906 earthquake. The displacements along roads, fences and railway tracks laid the foundation for the elastic rebound theory[*] propounded

---

[*] In geology, elastic rebound was the first theory to satisfactorily explain earthquakes. It explains how energy spreads during earthquakes. As rocks on opposite sides of a fault (believed to be stuck because of friction) are subjected to force, they accumulate energy and slowly deform until their internal strength is exceeded. At that time, a sudden movement occurs along the fault, releasing the accumulated energy, and the rocks snap back

by H.F. Reid, which provides the earliest scientific explanation for the mechanism of earthquakes.

Today we know that fault lines lie beneath many of the world's largest mountain ranges, like the Andes and the Himalayas, and that these faults occasionally move, giving rise to large earthquakes. The elastic rebound theory explains how energy is stored and released during earthquakes. It also reveals that the Earth's crust is not one continuous shell but broken up into several pieces with various shapes and geometries. The interactive movements of the plates generate huge amounts of stress around their margins, resulting in most earthquakes—this idea was ahead of time, even before the plate tectonic theory conceived in the 1960s.

The United States had experienced large earthquakes before the 1906 event. The December 1811 and February 1812 series of three large earthquakes of magnitude 7 to 7.8 near New Madrid, Missouri, revised later as moment magnitude, $M_w \leq 7.5$. The event caused bank failures along the Mississippi River, numerous landslides in Kentucky and Tennessee, and uplift and subsidence of large tracts of land in the Mississippi River floodplain. Although the sequence lasted for a year, curiously, it did not receive much attention for a long time despite the severity and extent of its impact. However, this earthquake laid the foundation for the science of paleoseismology, which was developed as an important tool to study prehistoric earthquakes. A monograph on the New Madrid earthquakes authored by Myron L. Fuller and published by the US Geological Survey in 1912[5] showcased co-seismic features like arching and doming of the ground and development of sandblows

---

to their original undeformed shape. Harry Fielding Reid proposed this theory from his observations of the 1906 San Francisco earthquake.

for the first time. These became fundamental expressions of ground shaking and liquefaction that occurred during large earthquakes.

Making of the Himalayas: A Cradle of Earthquakes

The Himalayas are the outcome of the ponderous movement generated by the upwelling of magma at the mid-oceanic ridge in the Indian Ocean. The world's highest peak, Mt Everest, stands about 8 km above sea level. The air is thin here, the land arid and temperatures extreme. It has been like this for a long time, much before humans existed on Earth. Hidden beneath the layers of rocks are marine plants and fossils. How did the marine fossils travel hundreds of kilometres from the closest sea at such altitudes? What happened to the sea that once hosted the rich marine life? Looking southwards and travelling back in time, say for about 225 million years, the mountains would be level with the ground and we would find ourselves being rafted back to Pangea. We would be standing on an island close to Antarctica and Australia, separated from the Asian continent by a vast ocean called the Tethys Sea. We would witness how Pangea broke up at around 200 Ma and the Indian subcontinent started its northward journey. After almost 120 million years of the journey, India would be just about 6400 km south of the Asian continent. Finally, it would ram into Eurasia about 40–50 million years ago. By then, India would have left Australia and Antarctica behind, and the Tethys Sea would have vanished. The remains of the geologically ancient Tethys Sea exist even in the summit of Mount Everest. The gray limestone deposited on the continental shelf of northern India, long before it began its northward journey, can be found in the Himalayas. These sedimentary rocks, formed in the Tethys Sea, are rich in fossils such as reefs and bivalves and indicate abundant and diverse tropical marine fauna. The collision would have slowed its northward motion to about half the speed but then the rapid uplift of the continental mass started. As the large landmasses have the same rock density, neither would dive down and they would form a collided range, forming the jagged peaks of the Himalayas.

As a result of spreading along the ridges, the Indian subcontinent started to move northwards about 100 million years ago. The millions of years of plodding at an estimated rate of 5 cm per year finally helped the Indian landmass ('plate') travel thousands of kilometres and slide under the Asian continent. The collisional stresses provided the forces to push up the Himalayan mountains and the Tibetan Plateau. As the collision and convergence of the two plates continue, the mountain is formed by a stack of thrust sheets scraped off the Indian crust and younger mountains and faults are generated.

The major thrust faults in the Himalayas are defined as Main Central Thrust (MCT), Main Boundary Thrust (MBT) and Main Frontal Thrust (MFT), from north to south, and progressively younger in the same direction. These major fault structures merge with the basement fault, which is defined as the detachment surface or the Main Himalayan Thrust (MHT), the surface on which the two converging plates are in contact. The various segments of the Himalayas—the sub-, lesser, great and Tethyan Himalayas—are marked by the elevation of these mountain ranges.

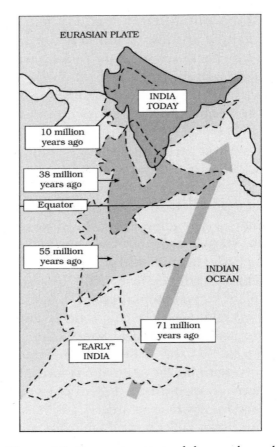

Figure 4.2: Reconstruction of the northward journey of the Indian plate.

Modern technologies such as GPS provide estimates of the current movement of the India–Eurasia plates. Part of the motion (about 20 of the 50 mm) is accommodated along the frontal part of the Himalayan mountain range, the MHT. The stress generated by this convergence is believed to be the source of great earthquakes—the 1803

Garhwal, 1905 Kangra, 1934 Bihar–Nepal, 1950 Assam, 2005 Kashmir and 2015 Nepal earthquakes among them. Recall that the great 1897 Shillong earthquake did not occur on this plate boundary, but it must have been influenced by the stresses generated along the Himalayas.

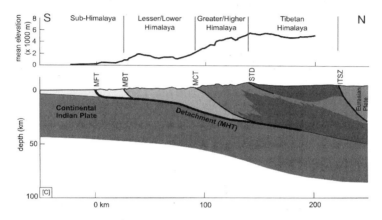

Figure 4.3: A pictorial cross-section of the Himalayas.

Great earthquakes along the Himalayas and other plate boundaries are attributed to stresses originating from plate motions. However, earthquakes occasionally occur within continental interiors, in the least expected locations. They strike like a bolt from the blue in areas with no known history of earthquakes and no mapped faults. The devastating earthquake (M_w 6.3), which occurred in September 1993 at Latur (Killari) was one such bolt from the blue. Located nearly 2000 km from the Himalayan plate boundary, this was not a place visited by earthquakes. As a region with no preparedness, the massive damage that followed took the lives of 10,000 people. Although of moderate magnitude, the 1993 Killari earthquake is one of the worst twentieth-century earthquakes in India. The only time an earthquake had become news in this region was in 1967 when a magnitude 6.7 earthquake occurred near Koyna, about 400 km west of the Killari earthquake. The Koyna quake, thought to have been induced by the nearby Sivajisagar Reservoir, is a widely quoted global example of a reservoir-triggered earthquake, discussed in some detail in the next chapter.

Earthquakes often lead to dramatic changes to the Earth's surface. Recall the narration in the beginning of this book about how the 1983 Central Idaho earthquake (M_w 6.9) stunned Lawana Knox on her elk-hunting trail as the target dropped 3 m when the fault ripped through the land that separated them. In addition to the visible ground movement, it can cause groundwater flow, landslides and mudflows. While some of these surface effects can be dramatic and long-lasting, many earthquakes are accompanied by changes that are subtle and not evident on the surface. In many instances, earthquakes occur on hitherto unmapped faults or blind faults that are not evident from the surface. Some earthquakes also cause secondary effects, such as landslides and liquefaction. Often wearing the garb of a detective, eager to solve the mystery of a murder and its perpetrator, a trained geologist can detect the footprints left by an earthquake.

Occasionally, the earthquake-related surface rupture could be a momentous event and affect the entire landscape. The 1819 earthquake in the Great Rann of Kutch was of the kind which raised a long stretch of land for several metres and dammed a river channel in the blink of an eye. The northern part of the block moved up along a fault, while the southern side sunk a few metres.

The changes were significant enough to affect the lives of the locals, who trade using the river and the hamlets supported by these water bodies. The forces that prompt the Earth to break into an occasional pirouette, as witnessed during the 1819 earthquake, require the investigators to understand earthquake physics thoroughly.

Examples testify that the Indian subcontinent has witnessed some of the most violent earthquakes globally. Almost 60 per cent are vulnerable to a shaking of great intensity (magnitude 7 and above). Based on seismic threat perception, India is geographically assigned four seismic zones—II, III, IV and V. Regions under zone V have the highest risk of damaging earthquakes and zone II is associated with the lowest level of seismicity. Over sixty-six active faults have been discovered in the country by the Geological Survey of India, and all are liable to produce earthquakes of various magnitudes. The Andaman–Nicobar subduction zone in the eastern Indian plate boundary is a belt of major earthquakes. Some also generate tsunamis, as exemplified by the great 2004 Andaman–Sumatra earthquake.

The Himalayan region extending for 2500 km in an east–west direction and the Andaman–Nicobar on the eastern seaboard, falling within seismic zone V, are the most susceptible to earthquakes exceeding magnitude 8.0. Most earthquakes occur along a well-defined belt running along the Himalayas. They spread to the northeast and further down the Andaman–Nicobar regions on the eastern seaboard. The Indian Oceanic plate is sliding under east Asia, and earthquakes in this region can also generate tsunamis. Although the last two centuries have witnessed five damaging earthquakes (magnitude greater or close to 8) striking the Himalayas and its outlying areas,

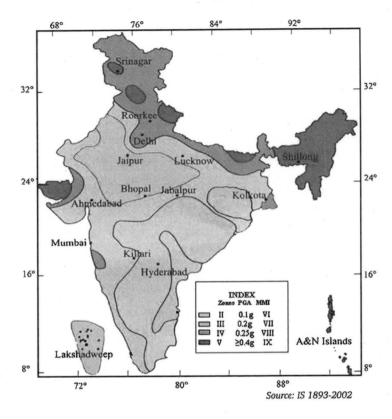

Figure 4.4: Seismic zonation map of India.

there have been no great earthquakes here since the 1950 Assam earthquake. This has been a concern since the plate motions have not stopped. Thus, most seismologists believe the Himalayan plate boundary is primed for the next massive quake. The 700-km-long segment between the 1905 Kangra and 1934 earthquakes has been identified as the most potent to create the next big one. This unbroken patch of the plate boundary is identified as a seismic gap or a space of current low-level activity. Perhaps the existence of this gap and the discussions about a potential gap-filling event make the citizens of Delhi and the neighbouring towns *nervous* every time they experience a small shock. We will learn more about Indian earthquakes as we move on with the story.

Foreshocks, Aftershocks and Swarms

Earthquakes occur when the accumulated stresses are released. They take place in different sequences and change the state of stress of the region. Post-earthquake, the system needs to regain its equilibrium and that is achieved through the production of aftershocks. These are smaller shocks that follow the main event. Aftershocks become less frequent with time, although they can continue for days, weeks, months or even years if the main shock is large. This sequence is not to be confused with swarm, composed mostly of small earthquakes with no identifiable main shock. Usually short-lived, they often recur at the same locations and are associated with fluid flow, volcanism, etc. Aftershocks follow the main earthquake and swarms do not herald an upcoming earthquake. However, there is another sequence named foreshocks. Although not omnipresent, foreshocks form part of the sequence that precede larger earthquakes in the same location.

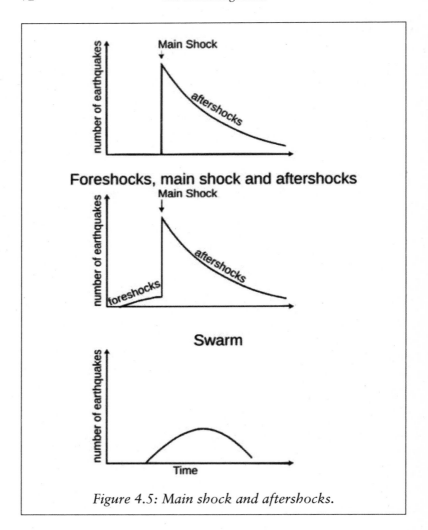

Figure 4.5: Main shock and aftershocks.

Chapter 5

Out-of-the-Blue Events

Once you have been in an earthquake you know, even if you survive without a scratch, that like a stroke in the heart, it remains in the earth's breast, horribly potential, always promising to return, to hit you again, with an even more devastating force.
—*Salman Rushdie,* The Ground Beneath Her Feet

In 1996, the authors Arch Johnston and Eugene S. Schweig used the famous lines by Winston Churchill, '. . . it is a riddle wrapped in a mystery inside an enigma', to qualify the New Madrid earthquake sequence of 1811–12.[1] While Churchill had been expressing his thoughts on the intentions and interests of Russia in 1939, the authors of the New Madrid paper were trying to convey that the twin sequence of earthquakes in the Mississippi Valley was equally puzzling and enigmatic. These large earthquakes originated in the central part of the North American plate. This region had no recorded history of earthquakes, unlike California in the western United States, but the 1811–12 sequence proved that eastern United States is not entirely free of earthquakes.

One could say that no part of the Earth is free from earthquakes. While there are several regions on the Earth where strong earthquakes occur frequently, there are many others characterized by infrequent or moderate earthquake activity. While plate boundaries are noted for larger and more frequent earthquakes, regions located far away from these boundaries are less productive. That does not mean that no earthquakes occur away from the plate boundaries in regions that seemingly appear aseismic. Earthquakes do occur in such interior regions of the continental plates, thousands of kilometers away from the plate boundaries. Distant from the plate boundaries and characterized by low rate of deformation, these regions are regarded as 'stable'. These regions, not involved in the current-day active tectonism, are designated as stable continental regions (SCRs). For example, the ~2500-km-long Himalayan Arc accommodates NNE-directed convergence of about ~35 mm/yr at the arc's western end in Kashmir and ~50 mm/yr at its eastern end near the Eastern Himalayas[2]. Compare this with the rate of convergence in Koyna (located more than 2000 km away from the plate boundary) where the rate of convergence is less 2 mm/year.[3] Slow deformation rate leads to slow stress build-up on the faults and lower seismic productivity hence the contrasting images of seismicity of the Himalaya and the peninsular India.

It follows from the above description that SCRs in general have not experienced any major tectonism currently or during the recent geologic history. In fact, geologic records testify that no significant tectonism would have occurred in the SCRs since the early Cretaceous-Paleogene Period.[*] Understandably, the SCRs have survived long in

---

[*] The Cretaceous Period is a geological time interval starting from 145 million years ago and ending around 66 million years ago. It is noted for the appearance of first flowering plants. During this interval, the Earth's land masses had assembled essentially into two continents,

the geologic history and are considered quite old (2.5–0.5 billion years). Nine continental-scale SCRs have been identified in Africa, Antarctica, Asia, Australia, China and North and South Americas. Unlike young and large active faults on the plate boundaries, those within SCRs are older and their segments are smaller in size, which means they cannot produce large or great earthquakes.

To understand how faults respond to stresses that originate from plate motions, one must relate to the properties of the rock system and how they respond to the stresses.[†] As the stress builds up and exceeds the frictional strength of the rocks, the blocks across the fault would slip, leading to a drop in stress which will build again. With the plate motions providing the driving power, it is easy to visualize the cycle of earthquakes or the relation between stress build-up and earthquakes.

Laurasia in the north and Gondwana in the south, which were almost completely separated by an equatorial sea called Tethys. The Cretaceous Period was followed by the Paleogene Period, which lasted from 66 to 23 million years. During the Paleogene Period, mammals evolved from relatively small, simple forms into a large group of diverse animals. By that time, South America, Antarctica, Australia, India and Africa were all separated out to become independent continental entities.

[†] Because of the friction and the rigidity of the blocks across a fault, they do not move past each other easily and remain locked. When stress builds up and exceeds the strength threshold, a rupture originates and during the earthquake the accumulated strain energy is released in part as seismic waves. The shear strength (τ) of large blocks involved in faulting is defined by a simple relation between the normal stress applied on the fault (σ_n) and the coefficient of friction (μ) by the relation ($\tau = \mu\sigma_n$).

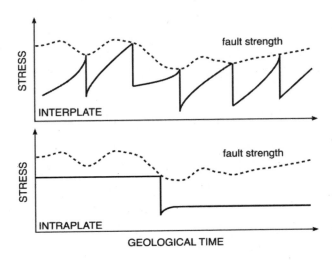

Figure 5.1: Stress changes in regions with different rates of tectonic loading.

Due to faster stress accumulation, earthquake recurrence period along the plate boundaries are shorter, falling in the range of ten to a few hundred years. On the contrary, within SCRs, where the stress build-up is much slower, earthquakes are fewer and the inter-event intervals are in the range of hundreds to thousands of years. More often, the intervals between the earthquakes are so long that the regions might not have any record of such events in their documented history. The lack of preparedness and a false sense of security in SCRs often lead to disproportionate damage as compared to the magnitude of the earthquake. The damage scenario worsens if the earthquake occurs in densely populated areas with poorly constructed buildings. The moderate magnitude earthquake of 30 September 1993, near Killari in the state of Maharashtra, a part of central India, is a classic example of how the perception of low-level seismic inactivity proved disastrous.

Figure 5.2: Global distribution of continental intraplate earthquakes.

The Killari earthquake is not an isolated event. Similar earthquakes have been reported from various continental regions. Kutch (western India), 1819; New Madrid (central United States), 1811–12; Charleston (south-eastern United States), 1886 are notable examples of SCR earthquakes. These earthquakes were not instrumentally recorded, but presumably they must have past histories of similar earthquakes. Therefore they make suitable candidates for geological investigations in the search for events in the past. Interest in investigating SCR earthquakes picked up after a series of earthquakes in the Australian interiors—1968 Meckering, 1986 Marryat Creek and 1988 Tennant Creek. The 'Christmas Day' earthquake of 1989, in a remote part of the Ungava Peninsula in northern Quebec, Canada, also spiked interest as it produced an 8.5 km long surface fault with a maximum displacement of 1.8 m. Interestingly, the main shock was preceded by a magnitude 5.1 foreshock ten hours earlier, although this was not recognized as a precursor. Indian SCR has generated earthquakes in rifted continental margins— the 1819 and 2001 earthquakes in the Kutch region are discussed in a later chapter. Earthquakes associated with ancient mid-continental rifts (Narmada,1997), non-rifted continental crust (Killari, 1993) and a reservoir-triggered earthquake of 1967 near the Koyna Dam form part of the following discussion.

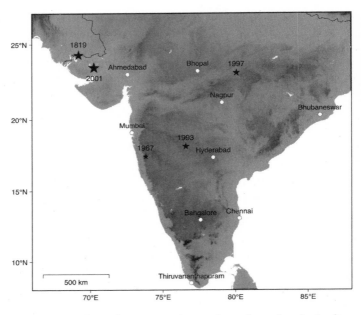

Figure 5.3: Significant continental earthquakes in India.

1993 Killari (Latur) Earthquake—An Unprecedented Event in the 'Aseismic' Central India

The year 1993 was a significant one for us, as practising earthquake researchers. On our return to India after the completion of our doctoral and postdoctoral studies in the United States by the end of July 1993, we were planning our research on the source of the 1819 Kutch earthquake. However, an earthquake of magnitude 6.3 rocked Killari in the heartland of the 'stable' Indian peninsular region a month later. It was surprising to experience an earthquake in an area considered low risk in the then seismic zonation map (see Figure 4.4 for the revised map in which the Killari region is included under Zone III; moderate damage risk zone).‡ That was the last day of the Ganesh Chaturthi festival, an important annual event in most parts of India. People had been celebrating the occasion. Celebrations had gone on past midnight, and people were fast asleep when the earthquake occurred at 3.56 a.m., both indoors and also outdoors, a habit among the local people. Most people sleeping indoors never woke up.

The small village of Killari is 42 km south of Latur, the district headquarters and one of Maharashtra's largest cities in the Marathwada region. The earthquakes claimed more than 10,000 human lives and reduced the village to rubble.[4] Nearly sixty-seven villages were destroyed. Another 700 villages in the Latur district and 600 in the Osmanabad district suffered damage. The World Bank actively supported the rehabilitation and reported that approximately 2,25,000 houses were destroyed or damaged, and more than 58,000 families were left homeless. Apart from extensive damage to homes, elevated water tanks, electricity and telecommunication systems were also affected. The total property loss was approximately US $333 million.[5]

---

‡ The seismic zonation map of India depicts the lowest, moderate and the most earthquake-prone areas in the country. It has been upgraded many times; the most recent revision was after the 1993 Killari earthquake. In the revised map, Zone I is omitted and Zones II and V represent regions of the lowest and highest risk. Earthquake intensities in these zones can vary from very strong to destructive shaking that is equivalent to a macro-seismic intensity scale, VI to IX or more.

Why did the earthquake cause so many deaths and severely damage homes? One reason is the time of the event in the early morning when people were fast asleep. The non-engineered style of construction of the village adobes was another important factor. The traditional houses typically have walls 4–5 feet thick, built with locally available stones in assorted shapes and sizes, cemented together by clay. Their roofs are made of wooden beams and light frames, overlain by layers of black soil. The walls of the houses are of random thickness, and small cavities made within them serve as safe lockers for cash, jewellery and other valuables. The walls and heavy roofs collapsed during the earthquake, crushing the people who were inside. As one surveys the layout of these houses, one cannot miss the socially determined designs. Here, the communities live as extended families, and parents live with their married sons while the daughters move to their husband's houses after marriage. As new members are added, and the families grow, houses are often expanded laterally, without any coherent structural designs, often ignoring any concerns about safety. As this region had no documented history of earthquakes, guarding against earthquake damage was obviously not a consideration in the design of these homes.

The lingering fear and the Marathi film 3:56 Killari

When we visited Killari soon after the earthquake, a part of the prosperous 'Sugar Belt of India', as it was known, was a deserted heap of rubbles. Large areas of sunflower fields ready for harvest looked abandoned, and in most cases, their owners were dead. Grieving relatives talked of the times they had spent on the farm and their hopes for a high yield that year. There was despair everywhere.

Someone we met there asked us if the souls of those who meet an untimely death return as ghosts. We may not believe so, but most people believe that eerie vestiges of the deceased souls or 'ghosts' of the earthquake victims still haunt their beautiful village.

Claims of ghosts of disaster victims visiting their neighbourhoods are not a new experience for survivors. The survivors of Japan's traumatic 2011 earthquake and tsunami, which killed more than 15,000 people, reported sighting restless spirits of the victims known as 'tsunami ghosts'. The traumatized survivors admitted to seeing victims' faces in puddles, wandering on the beaches and appearing at their doors. Such experiences are shared by survivors of many disaster hit areas. British reporter Richard Lloyd Parry's book, *Ghosts of the Tsunami*, and 'Tsunami Spirits', an episode from volume 2 of Netflix's *Unsolved Mysteries* released in 2020, have featured similar mysterious personal experiences that are difficult to rationalise. Neuroscientists think these visual or audio hallucinations provide emotional strength and comfort and reduce feelings of isolation in survivors.

Nearly three decades after the horrifying event, the local people believe that the ghosts of the victims still return to their villages. The Marathi film *3:56 Killari*, released in 2015, tells the story of a fourteen-year-old girl's journey to learn about the mysteries of her past life. The protagonist of the film, an earthquake survivor, now an adolescent girl, experiences mysterious flashes as she visits the village. Her parents were killed in the earthquake, and her later years were spent with her grandparents. She cannot wipe out the horrific images; they come alive every time she visits the village through the spirits that haunt the place. Memories of death and fear do not fade away. Even now, residents of

Killari village observe 'black day' on 30 September. Even today, they recall the day with fear and some sleep outside their houses.

Dr Ashok Potdar, a resident of Killari who practised medicine there since 1976, shared his experience with the *Financial Express*.[6] After a hectic day of work, he had just retired to bed, and the earthquake woke him up to darkness, death and destruction. His hospital building, made of bricks, survived with cracks. He was safe, but he lost fourteen extended family members. Among the youngest survivors of the earthquake who would not recall anything from that fateful morning is Aarti Kapelkar, who was just one-and-a-half months old then. Little Aarti was sleeping with her parents, and she was stuck in the debris of their house. She and her mother survived, but her father died. Arati is a true survivor who, along with her widowed mother, struggled to complete her studies and currently works as a teacher. Ashok Potdar and Aarti Kapelkar are living examples that show how the 1993 earthquake must have impacted the social and psychological lives of the survivors. All of them say one thing: 'We did not expect an earthquake here. Why is it that no one told us?'

Why Was the 1993 Earthquake Totally Unexpected?

As we read earlier, plate boundaries have distinctive topographic features created by tectonic activity including earthquakes. For example, look at the 40-million-year-old Himalayas—a geologically young and tectonically active mountain chain. Along the Himalayan range, the topography is rugged and its landforms such as steep hills and deep gorges suggest youthfulness, geologically speaking. It would be evident how the tectonic activity in the region have shifted river courses and carved morphological features that bear signatures of ground movements. Youthful rivers cut deep valleys fringed by staircase-like terraces formed by tectonism and erosion. Fault lines and other geologic evidence of past ground movements can be found everywhere as we travel through the Himalaya. Over time, erosion modifies landscapes, but if the tectonic signatures develop at rates faster than the rates at which erosion can wipe them out, the landforms are preserved. Thus, the features created by this young mountain chain testifies that it is an 'earthquake country'.

Heading south to the nearly 3.4-billion-year-old Indian peninsula, we find no young growing mountains. We would travel through the flat terrain, created by millions of years erosion which would have wiped out any tectonic signatures of its distant past. However, there is one distinctive geomorphologic feature, one of its youngest landforms—the Deccan plateau. Plate tectonic reconstruction tells us that India separated from Madagascar about 88 million years ago and began its northward journey. Soon after the transit started, India passed over a volcanic hotspot east of Madagascar, now an island called Reunion, occupies that spot. A huge eruption of this hotspot 65 million years ago is thought to have laid down the Deccan Traps, a vast bed of basalt lava that covers part of central India and opened a rift, which separated India from the Seychelles plateau. The largest among the volcanic features on Earth, the Deccan Traps cover 500,000 sq. km of the west-central Indian subcontinent. The flat-lying stacks of basalt flows have produced a staircase-like elevated topography in the Deccan region. There are no surface offset features that would suggest presence of any recent faulting episodes.

Now, let us zoom into the epicentral zone of the Killari earthquake. The earthquake originated in the Tirna River basin, which is located at an elevation of about 0.5 km from the mean sea level. The region presents a flat landscape, with no topographic highs more than 50 m above the broad valley. Over millions of years since its creation, the low level of tectonism and high erosional rate are believed to have shaped this gently rolling and relatively featureless terrain. The 1993 earthquake left a break on the ground, a subtle expression of the underlying fault. The discontinuous crack in the ground traversed agricultural fields for about 2 km and formed a minor hump, not more than 80 cm high. Villagers noted these breaks in the ground, which they described as 'the upward movement of the soil as if someone has tilled the ground'. Very soon, these subtle features were levelled by rain. That is not surprising, given the subtilty of the features caused by the earthquake and the tropical weather conditions. If earthquakes create large vertical or horizontal displacements and if they return in a few hundreds of years, the signatures would be perceptible. However, if a 'once-in-a-blue moon' event creates an 80 cm high mount which gets eroded in the next season of rains, obviously there will be no topographic signatures left. The subtle nature of surface deformation created by the 1993 earthquake, and the rarity of earthquakes here explain why this landscape is devoid of any tectonic signatures. People living in the area neither have any prior experience nor have they heard of earthquakes from their ancestors. Any past event must have occurred centuries before humans started to occupy this place, thus there are no mentions of Killari-type earthquakes in historical records. The history of the region does not mention any significant earthquake activity in the region. Instrumentally recorded earthquake data also do not suggest any notable seismic activity in this region. Thus, there were no reasons to suspect that a devastating earthquake could occur here. Naturally, with this deceptive perception, the level of preparedness was also very low.

However, it appears that the ground had been getting ready to rupture. The silence was being disturbed by a few rumblings. The seismological observatory at Hyderabad recorded twenty-six tremors of magnitude more than 2.0 from this region during October–November 1992.[7] These were small shocks, and they eventually stopped, with no anticipation of any larger earthquake. However, the locals reported blast-like sounds, which scientists attributed to their shallow depths (about 5 km). But why did the scientists not perceive them as forerunners of a future event? The small shocks did not ring an alarm in a region of low background seismicity with no mapped tectonic features. After the magnitude 4.5 earthquake of 18 October 1992, the largest in a series of small tremors, D.T. Kamble, a geologist at the Geological Survey of India, surveyed the region. He reported damage to houses in many villages, including Killari, where the effects appeared to be maximum. Interestingly, when the earthquake occurred on 30 September 1993, the seismologists found that the source of the main shock was very close to Killari. Although Kamble's report recommended close monitoring of the region, it was struck by a heavily damaging earthquake about ten months after the October 1992 foreshock before any such plans could materialize.

The next important issue before the seismologists was to trace the history of earthquakes in Killari and the surrounding regions. In fact, the southern peninsular India is not completely free of earthquakes, but due to the low-level activity, it did not receive a high priority in instrumental recording. Thus, any small or moderate events that might have occurred in the region are documented with its location and intensity, based on press reports. Given the lack of instrumental monitoring and inter-event intervals, which may run into thousands of years as against the period of documented history, there is a possibility that many past earthquakes may not be reported. Thus, we go back to the early pages of history and beyond, looking for any information relating to earthquake occurrence.

Faint memories of earthquakes: Pages from the past

A search of the earthquake catalogues for peninsular India indicate that no significant earthquakes of magnitude greater than 6.0 have occurred in the source zone of the Killari event during recent or historical times. The region was seismically inactive, except for a few events of intensity III to IV. However, a 400 km long, north-west-oriented corridor in which at least five events of intensity IV occurred during the past 150 years was identified only after the 1993 earthquake. Only a small part of this zone was activated in 1993, and the status of the rest of this structure is unclear. Earthquakes of comparable sizes are unlikely to have occurred here before 1993, at least for the past 1000 years. This assumption is based on our observation of the long-standing historical monuments dating back to 1000–1200 CE in the region that had remained intact until 1993.

Although the Killari region had not experienced any significant earthquakes for at least 1000 years, there were older events in the area. A 1500-year-old earthquake was reported from the location called Ter, 70 km north-west of Killari. In the continental interiors, the repeat time of earthquakes may be very long, which is not surprising given the lack of active tectonism. But there could be locations in the continental interior regions where earthquakes

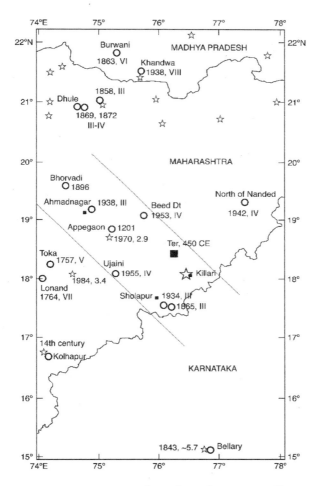

Figure 5.4: Historical earthquakes near Killari.

must have occurred far beyond history. With no human experience of such events, the prolonged quiescence may be perceived as a signal of permanent dormancy. These peculiarities of the SCR regions make their seismic hazard assessment very challenging.

Much of the state of Maharashtra sits on thick deposits of volcanic rocks that were deposited more than 60 million years ago. The sheets of dark-coloured rocks that solidified from molten lava are called basalt and vary in thickness from a few tens of meters to almost 2 km at some locations. The lava was deposited over the rigid and tectonically stable peninsular shield which formed 3.8 to 2.5 billion years ago. The hard basement beneath the basalts carries its own signatures of past tectonism, that are not observable on the surface. For example, geophysical (gravity) surveys suggest that the basement is marked by tectonic structures such as ridges and basins. Global studies suggest that ancient tectonic structures that must have formed millions of years ago in SCRs can be reactivated to generate earthquakes. The epicentral zone of the 1993 earthquake is located on the flanks of a NW–SE trending subterranean structure expressed as a gravity high. Geologists argue that these are expressions of earlier faulting episodes, which form weak zones and their reactivation could lead to 1993-type earthquakes. Interestingly, historical earthquakes in the region, although few and far between seem to follow the same regional trend. The small surface break and the historical records of past earthquakes prompted geologists to explore the region in their search for any evidence of earthquakes beyond history. Geological evidence obtained in trenches excavated in the rupture zone of the 1993 earthquake suggests a previous event might have occurred here thousands of years ago. Thermoluminescence (TL) method,[§] widely used to date soil samples, yielded an age of about 17,000 years for the previous faulting episode.

[§] The thermoluminescence (TL) method of dating measures the amount of light emitted from energy stored in certain rock types and soils to obtain an absolute date for a specific event that occurred in the past. The method is a direct dating technique, meaning that the amount of energy emitted is a direct result of the event being measured.

This age, obtained by the authors of this book, from a single trench is insufficient to reliably determine the age of the event. More studies are required to determine the ages of past earthquakes.

The rarity of the Killari earthquake and its unprecedented economic and social impact created an awakening among the practitioners of science and administrative officials. The scientific interest was primarily due to its occurrence in a region considered relatively free from damaging earthquakes. On the administrative side, the Government of Maharashtra designed the Maharashtra Emergency Earthquake Rehabilitation Project (MEERP), an agency which attempted to rebuild housing on a massive scale and retrofit damaged buildings and infrastructure. The team, led by the union and state governments, included many players from non-governmental organizations (NGOs), World Bank, Department for International Development (DFID), United Nations Development Program (UNDP) and Asian Development Bank (ADB). The Department of Science and Technology (DST), Government of India instituted a consortium of research institutes led by the National Geophysical Research Institute (NGRI), Hyderabad and India Meteorology Department (IMD), New Delhi. An International Advisory Committee and a National Steering Committee were set up to advise the government on technical matters, including upgradation of the seismic monitoring network. Following the 1993 earthquake, most stations of the national seismological network were upgraded from analog to digital. Several new stations were also added to the national seismic network, enhancing the detection level of earthquakes.

The rehabilitation and reconstruction efforts and the World Bank-assisted programme implemented by the Maharashtra government made significant advances.

Repair, retrofitting and construction of 2,25,000 houses, public and community infrastructure facilities, and social rehabilitation programmes contributed to rebuilding the villages. By following simple and cost-effective earthquake-resistant features for new constructions and retrofitting the existing structures, the residents' houses were now safe. The process also helped train several local artisans in earthquake-resistant building techniques. The Killari earthquake led to the revision of the seismic zonation map of the country, which was redrawn to indicate that the low seismicity indicated by Zone I could be a misnomer. A new zonation map, deleting Zone I, was created (see Figure 4.4). In summary, the Killari earthquake served as a wake-up call to recognize the underestimated seismic hazard in regions located far from plate boundaries. Not surprisingly, the 1993 earthquake created such renewed interest in SCR earthquakes that the American Geophysical Union (AGU) chose it as a theme for the 1998 Chapman Conference held in Hyderabad, India. Killari has been quiet since the 1993 earthquake, but other regions in the Indian subcontinent seem to have been awakened.

Earthquakes along the Narmada–Son Lineament

In less than four years, after the Killari earthquake, on 22 May 1997, the city of Jabalpur in Madhya Pradesh, was rocked by an earthquake of magnitude M_W 5.8. It was as if SCR India was warming up for more earthquakes after the Killari event. The occurrence of this temblor reinforced the hitherto underestimated seismic vulnerability in peninsular India. The increased seismic instrumentation, including a state-of-the-art recording station near Jabalpur, made it possible to investigate various aspects of this earthquake and its relation to the tectonic structures. The Jabalpur earthquake is the first moderate SCR event in India that was analysed using digital records. Interestingly, the 1997 earthquake is spatially associated with a prominent structure that cuts across central India in an NNE–SSW direction known as the Narmada-Son Lineament/Fault (NSL). The NSL was not quietly cutting through the continent; it has been seismically active since historical times. In addition to the clear spatial association with a well-mapped fault, focal depths of the NSL earthquakes are found to be very deep, closer to the Moho.¶ The focal depth of the Jabalpur earthquake is ~40 km, and in contrast to the Killari earthquake, the damage was considerably much lower. Yet, 8546 houses collapsed and 52,690 were badly damaged. The earthquake affected 887 villages, leaving thirty-eight dead and 350 injured.[8]

How Jabalpur woke up to a quake unprepared

The magnitude 5.8 earthquake was sourced near Amanpur, 25 km south-east of Jabalpur city. This was another early morning event (4.20 a.m.) that occurred when people were indoors. The district of Jabalpur was the worst affected as most of the casualties took place there. Thousands of people were rendered homeless and had to be evacuated to relief camps. The National Centre for Earthquake Engineering at the Indian Institute of Technology, Kanpur observed the seismic response of modern buildings in and around Jabalpur, which was used to evaluate seismic preparedness. They also offered their expertise in repairing seismically damaged structures. The maximum intensity of

---

¶ The boundary between the Earth's crust and its mantle, the Moho, lies at a depth of about 35 km below continents and about 7 km beneath the oceanic crust.

shaking experienced during the earthquake was found to
be VIII, with strong variations across locations. The poor
performance of buildings was mostly attributed to the
shortcomings of their design.

Unlike the Killari region, the Narmada rift has been
moderately active throughout the documented history.
Over thirty earthquakes ranging from magnitude 3 to
6.5 have occurred here in the last seventy years. Among
these historical events, the Satpura earthquake (at 40 km)
was the deepest. While there is no documented history of
any large earthquakes in central India, Alex Copley and
co-workers interpret the regional morphological features
as fault scarps. The morphological cues on fault scarps
indicate the presence of active faults in the region. They
present evidence for past earthquakes of magnitude
7.6–8.4 in the western Tapti region of the Narmada rift.[9]
The spatial distribution of earthquakes in the Narmada
rift defines a well-organized spatial association with the
tectonic structure.

The association of earthquakes with well-developed
tectonic features is a rarity in SCR regions. That rarity can
be explained by applying the tenets of the plate tectonic
theory. It has been documented in the textbooks of geology
that during its evolution, the Narmada region was subjected
to both compression and extension. The geological clock
needs to be turned back to hundred million years ago to
reimagine the continental configuration at that time. We
must visualize how continental masses were drifting around
and colliding with each other. During periods of early
stages of continental formation, crustal blocks had accreted
and were drifting around and colliding with each other.
As they collided, the individual continental blocks got
fused. This agglomeration of three ancient landmasses—
the Dharwar, Aravalli and Singhbhum—occurred about

3.5 billion years ago. There was a crustal extension or stretching and profuse volcanic and magmatic activity till about 66–56 million years ago. The collision with the Eurasian plate front also marked an end to the tectonic processes associated with the stretching of crust or lithosphere. All these extensional and compressional tectonic processes have left their imprints, and occasional small to moderate earthquakes continue to occur on these ancient structures.

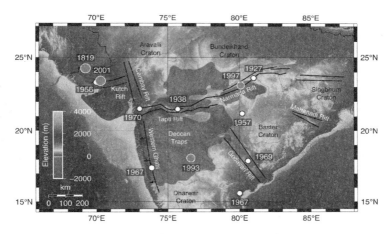

Figure 5.5: Cratons and paleo-rifts inherited from past tectonics. Important earthquakes are marked.

Earthquakes in Koyna: The Work of a Reservoir

Whether or not human activities cause earthquakes is a frequently asked question. The answer is yes, and there are ample examples of small and occasional moderate earthquakes triggered by mining, fluid injection, reservoir filling, etc. Among various types of anthropogenic seismic activity, earthquakes triggered by large artificial reservoirs are significant. Perhaps it started with the case of the Hoover Dam impounded on the Colorado River, in the United

States to make Lake Mead. Earthquakes occurred here in 1945, and the number of earthquakes increased as the water level started to rise. Seismicity associated with reservoirs has been documented globally—in the Americas, Canada, Africa, China. Harsh K. Gupta and other researchers at the National Geophysical Research Institute, Hyderabad have done pioneering studies on reservoir triggered earthquakes.[10]

The earthquake of magnitude M_W 6.3 that shook Koyna in Maharashtra considered a classic example of reservoir-triggered seismicity. The earthquake killed about 200 people and destroyed the Koyna township. From the studies that followed, it was learnt that the area's residents had had no prior experience of earthquakes, like what we saw in the case of the 1993 Killari earthquake. After the reservoir was filled in 1962, people started to feel some rumblings, which developed as a devastating event on 10 December 1967. It was preceded by a magnitude 5.5 event on 13 September of the same year. The earthquake activity that picked up since then has not ceased, although no earthquake of comparable magnitude of the 1967 event repeated here. The commissioning of the Warna Reservoir in 1985, which is located south of Koyna, has only added to the on-going frequency of earthquakes. The continuing seismicity of the region for more than half a century demonstrates a clear temporal relation with reservoir filling.

One may wonder why only a few reservoirs trigger earthquakes. For example, some of the largest dams in the world have not triggered any earthquakes while some smaller ones have. The processes that lead to reservoir-triggered earthquakes are explained by a favourable combination of the local geological conditions and the nature of reservoir filling. A reservoir would introduce stress changes in its vicinity due to its weight. This could weaken the pre-existing fault that is already close to the tipping point. Further, the increase in pore fluid pressure due to reservoir filling within the rocks also weakens the faults. Global case studies suggest that presence of faults that are close to slippage and the rate of filling are important factors. In Koyna, there must have been faults that would have generated earthquakes in the long run even without a reservoir, as we saw in Killari, where a dormant fault, located in another part of the basalt terrain (Deccan plateau) got activated on its own.

The earthquake phenomena in Koyna demonstrates a strong correlation of seismicity with the annual reservoir loading. Refilling happens after monsoon, during the months of June–July. The frequency of earthquakes increases after September and continues through November and December. This delay of two to three months is the time taken for the pore pressure to reach the depths of about 2–3 km where earthquakes originate. Analyses of years of filling history at Koyna suggest that a rate of 2 m/week provides a threshold to trigger earthquakes. In other words, in a region that is already weak, the effect of a reservoir is like the last straw on the camel's back. While most global examples of triggered earthquakes show a tendency to gradually taper off, Koyna remains active, even half a century after the initial seismic activity, which makes it a special case among reservoir triggered earthquakes. It still generates occasional earthquakes of magnitude around 4 or more. And the yearly pattern persists, although the frequency of earthquakes and their magnitudes are getting lower—a global rarity in the reservoir-triggered earthquakes. Such has been the interest about Koyna that a deep-drilling project has been commissioned to understand more about the mechanism of earthquakes here. The Koyna and Killari earthquakes can be considered as

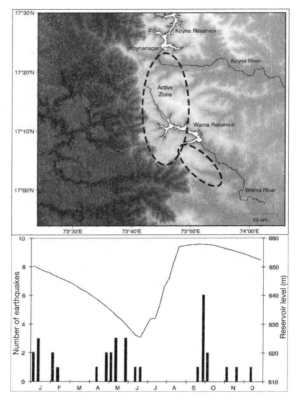

Figure 5.6: (Top) *Monthly frequency of earthquakes near Koyna and Warna Reservoirs;* (bottom) *Average lake levels in the Koyna Reservoir during 1983, considered as a representative year.*

'out-of-the-blue' events, occurring in an apparently stable continental interior, but earthquake preparedness is a must even in such areas where nature can be the most capricious.

❖ ❖ ❖

Earthquakes in the Vicinity of Artificial Reservoirs

Natural (precipitation, snow melt, etc.) and anthropogenic (dams, fluid injections, etc.) processes lead to an increase in pore pressure and cause earthquakes, a phenomenon referred to as hydroseismicity. Earthquakes occur by diffusion of fluid pressure to fault zones which are already critically stressed, such that a slight change would lead to slip on weak faults. Research at the Nurek Reservoir (Tajikistan) showed that the rate of loading in the reservoir is a critical factor. The most compelling seismic evidence in support of fluid pressure related earthquakes is their observed space–time pattern near injection wells. It is noted that the frequency of earthquakes increases and spreads out when there is injection. The physical basis for fluid induced faulting is expressed by the failure equation $\tau = c + \mu\sigma - \rho$, here '$\tau$' is the existing shear stress on a fracture or a fault plane, 'μ' is the frictional coefficient, 'σ' is the normal stress acting of the fault plane and 'ρ' is the pore pressure within the rock system. An increase in pore pressure would decrease the normal stress (right hand side of the failure equation). This would increase the shear stress acting on the fault (left side of the equation), eventually causing earthquakes. It is to be noted that a reservoir does not create a fault, it only causes a slip on an existing weak fault. A small change would be the tipping point.

In the case of reservoirs, the stratum beneath gets weaker though multiple processes. As the load in the reservoir increases, it influences the rocks below.

First, the effect of the load would increase the normal stress and the fault would become unstable. Next, there is an increase in pore pressure within the rock matrix, caused by the squeezing effect of the load. Later, diffusion will transmit pore pressure to larger areas and cause more earthquakes.[11] David Simpson and his co-workers have defined these processes as rapid and delayed responses of reservoirs. They later proposed that 'triggered' rather than 'induced' is a better description of the process, clarifying that earthquakes are triggered only where conditions are favourable. The frequency and magnitude of triggered earthquakes reduces gradually as the hydromechanical environment around the reservoir attains stability. Only five reservoirs have generated earthquakes of magnitude more than 6.0 globally and about fifty have caused earthquakes of magnitude 4 to 5.9.

Chapter 6

The Mound of God

The earthquake, however, must be to everyone a most impressive event: the earth, considered from our earliest childhood as the type of solidity, has oscillated like a thin crust beneath our feet; and in seeing the laboured works of man in a moment overthrown, we feel the insignificance of his boasted power.

—Charles Darwin

On a cold morning in December 1997, as we stood on the salt-encrusted surface of the Great Rann of Kutch, all we could hear was the wind whistle and a crackle under the ground where we were standing. It was a desolate landscape stretching far and wide, all the way to the distant horizon. It would be flooded during the monsoons, when the tidal currents from the Gulf of Kutch flow onto this white desert, transforming it into an inland sea. Flamingos would soon arrive for breeding, and the marshes would turn green, teeming with life. As the monsoon retreats, the waters recede, leaving behind an endless stretch of snowy flats encrusted with crystals of salt. The landscape was captivating, worth endless photography, but we had to start our work. A topographic survey to map the Allah

Bund morphology, the most important vestige of the 1819 earthquake, was to begin soon.

We were at the Border Security Force (BSF) outpost at Vigakot near the India–Pakistan border. That is where we were to stay, sharing meals with the jawans and sleeping in the bunkers. Sunset is a spectacular sight in the Rann, and the warm day slipped gradually into a calm, breezy night. This fantastic land of nothingness played host to a large earthquake on 16 June 1819. We were on the trail of that event. Our rendezvous with the Rann of Kutch had begun.[1]

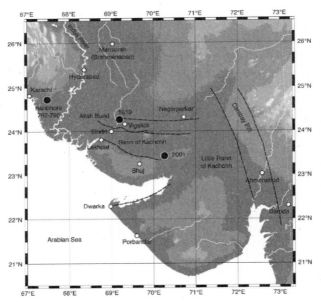

Figure 6.1: Rann of Kutch and adjoining regions showing the tectonic features.

It was a new experience in a different kind of land. The large area of salt marshes called the Rann of Kutch (also spelled Kachchh) stretches across the border between India and Pakistan. Much of the Rann is in the Kutch district of Gujarat and extends to Sindh in Pakistan. Extending in east-westerly direction and occupying around 26,000 sq. km, the Rann of Kutch is divided into the Great and Little Rann. This 'marsh of alluvium' is home to India's most extensive salt plains. This spectacular landscape that shimmers under a blazing sun and sparkles under a moonlit sky remain less explored, even by tourists. To its north lies the Thar Desert, and to its south extend the hills of Kutch. The Indus River Delta lies to its west.

Home to exotic flora and fauna, the Little Rann may give us the occasional company of the wild ass, a protected species that owns a sanctuary here. Herds of camels pass by, unconcerned about human interferences. They walk to the nearest water body and would be lucky if a mirage did not deceive them. 'Do not be deluded by the mesmerizing beauty of the Rann,' our friend, the BSF chief would caution us. 'On this vast and featureless Rann, you might get lost, cross the international border, and end up in Pakistan.' He then narrates the story of one of his camels. She got into an 'international affair' with a male across the border and walked over, only to be brought back rather unceremoniously. We set out to explore the land. One task was to document the landscape changes and map the Allah Bund. The other was to explore the region for evidence of any previous earthquake that may have shaken the area. They might be documented in history or preserved in the geological record.

Trail of the Allah Bund Earthquake

The evening of 16 June 1819 was unlike any other in Kutch and the southern parts of Sindh. At around 6.50 p.m., the sunset was as spectacular as ever. Captain Mac Murdo, who was posted as a British Political Resident stationed in Bhuj at the time, described the pre-earthquake dawn as 'a day that had been cool and showery; Fahrenheit's thermometer ranging from 81° to 85°. The monsoon had set in mildly . . . The wind . . . had been blowing pleasantly towards evening . . .' Then came the earthquake, described as:

> The first and greatest shock took place on the 16th of June 1819, a few minutes before seven in the evening. The wind, which had been blowing pleasantly towards evening at the commencement of the concussion fell into a dead calm, and in a moment, all was consternation and horror. The wretched inhabitants of Bhooj were flying in all directions. A heavy appalling noise—the violent undulatory motion of the ground—the crash of the buildings—and the dismay and terror which appeared in every countenance produced a sensation horrible beyond description. The shock lasted from two to three minutes, and during that short period, the city of Bhooj was almost levelled with the ground . . . The devastation was general throughout Kutch . . .[2]

Descriptions about the earthquake are available in Mac Murdo's report. The earthquake originated in the northern part of the Rann, but the damage was severe in distant cities. It also did something quite unusual to the ground. It uplifted the northern fringes of the Rann and formed a mound that blocked the Nara River, a distant distributary of the Indus that used to flow through the Rann to the Gulf of Kutch. It was used as a trade route by coastal and inland merchants in the Sindh Province. The immediate vicinity of the earthquake was not highly populated but the event caused extensive damage. The brick fort in Vigakot, a tax collection centre at that time, collapsed.

The maximum impact was felt within a 70 km radius around the epicentre. About 7000 houses were destroyed, and more than 1500 people died in the cities of Bhuj and Anjar. About 300 km from the epicentre, in Ahmedabad, the ground shook severely and the spire of a 450-year-old mosque toppled. It was the first historically known large earthquake that impacted human settlements of the region and their supporting infrastructures, including waterways and tax-collection centres. Following the quake, a sudden rush of water from the ocean inundated the region, limiting the mobility of people. The earthquake caused significant changes in the fluvial systems. It was reported that in the districts south of Hyderabad, the flow stopped in several channels for three days after the earthquake.

Figure 6.2: Allah Bund viewed from the east.

The day after the earthquake, the local people woke up to an unbelievable sight. Along the northern fringes of the Rann, they saw a mound that had sprung up during the earthquake. The mound, rising 2–4 m off the ground and stretching from east to west, was a sight to behold. The natives named it the *Allah Bund*—the mound of God.

It was silhouetted against the low hills of the distant Nagar Parker ridge. This spectacular landscape stretched for more than 60 km, extending to Pakistan. A new lake had also formed near Vigakot. It still remains and if one were to follow a herd of camels in the area moving in search of water, the trail would lead to this lake created in 1819.

The Allah Bund transformed our textbook knowledge of earthquake-sculpted landforms into an awe-inspiring real-time experience. For any visitor, it was impossible to avoid reflecting on the landscape sculpted by the 1819 earthquake. Charles Lyell believed the event marked a watershed movement in the history of seismology and used it as a classic example to describe surface deformation caused by earthquakes. To borrow the words of Simon Winchester, it 'presented a distant prospect of where forces of the world were at work, a place of an elemental significance, and a disastrous place once—these days quiet again, serenely biding its time'.[3]

After the international border came into existence, part of the mound would extend to Pakistan. The lack of logistics, incident weather and the proximity to an international border must have kept the researchers at bay. Nearly 180 years had passed after the earthquake when we landed there, aided by hand-held GPS receivers and digital theodolite[*] to map the mound. Running roughly parallel to the border, although eroded at some locations creating deep gullies, one can walk over this elevated structure. The

---

[*] Digital theodolite, the modern version of theodolite, is a surveying instrument for measuring both horizontal and vertical angles. It uses a telescope movable within a perpendicular axis—the horizontal and the vertical. It is a key tool in surveying and engineering work. It can be used to create elevation profiles across ground features and make an elevation map of the target areas.

face of the mound, or the 'scarp', stands 5 m above ground level in some places where it is not levelled by erosion.

After the 1819 earthquake, which dramatically demonstrated the relationship between earthquakes and the formation of fault scarps, faulting was regarded as a primary tenet in earthquake science. Charles Lyell, the author of *The Principles of Geology*, was the first among the scholars who could appreciate the causal links of level changes to movement along fault blocks triggering earthquakes based on this example. The north-dipping fault created by the earthquake did not reach the surface, but the ground was raised as a scarp. Towards the south of the scrap, warping caused the land to sink by a few meters. These land transformations demonstrated what geologists describe as 'coseismic' surface deformation.[†] The earthquake also produced many secondary features, such as liquefaction. The sandblows formed by liquefaction are still preserved in various parts of the Rann. All of these phenomena were new to geologists at the time.

The Sinking Fort of Sindri

The Sindri Fort, a revenue outpost downstream of the Nara River and an important landmark in the region has been used for a long time as a proxy to describe coseismic subsidence. The fort, located ~8 km south of the Allah Bund, reportedly submerged a few hours after the earthquake, and

---

[†] When rocks are stressed, it can deform by bending or faulting and this is a permanent change. Rocks deform simultaneously with the earthquake, which is described as coseismic. The large fault breaks created by an earthquake is an example of coseismic deformation. Some large earthquakes cause surface elevation changes, leading to coseismic subsidence or uplift.

the area was converted to an inland lake that extended for
25 km. People who took asylum in this lone tower that was
reportedly standing had to be rescued in boats the next day.
Lyell writes, '. . . neither the rush of the sea into this new
depression, nor the movement of the earthquake, threw
down entirely the small fort of Sindree, one of the four
towers, the northwestern, still continuing to stand; and, the
day after the earthquake, the inhabitants who had ascended
to the top of this tower, saved themselves in boats'.[4]

Figure 6.3: View of the Sindri Fort after the earthquake.

To clarify his statement, Lyell presented pre- and post-
woodcut prints of the Sindri Fort. Early surveys attributed
the submergence of the Sindri Fort at the foundation level
to subsidence of the land by ~1–3 m, due to downfaulting
during the earthquake, and Lyell considered it strong
evidence of land-level changes created by earthquakes.

Lyell wanted to use such examples of surface-faulting
earthquakes to strengthen the theory of uniformitarianism,

which proposed that mountains and valleys were formed in prehistoric times by omnipresent geological forces and not by 'one-time' cataclysmic events. The pillars of the Temple of Serapis (an Egyptian deity worshipped by the Romans) raised above the ground by the Earth's internal forces was another case he used. By citing the presence of marine organisms that could not have lived above the low-tide level, Lyell made a deductive inference that the lower part of Serapis columns had emerged from water, facilitated by some natural forces. For Lyell, these level changes that would elevate the land are small steps (a quantum, as the physicist would say) in the long process of building a mountain.

Walking over the Allah Bund: A Geologist's Dream

Peering into the darkness and silent nights in Kutch—a theatre of war in 1965 between India and Pakistan—one could think of the people who lost their lives in that war. The BSF soldiers with whom we shared the bunker enjoyed telling us stories they had heard from their senior colleagues. The transmission of stories continues unbroken, and, as they pass through each narrator, the stories develop wings. They took us to a distant and secluded area where human skeletons remain exposed as the desert winds lift the soil. This is the abode of the ghosts, and they resurrect and move around in the night. Apparitions that may belong to the ghosts of those war victims appear to be walking at night, the soldiers say. One sure way of knowing their route is the flashing light that looks like the flickering of the fireflies. We spotted them, too, distant and disappearing into the darkness. The sceptical ghost sighters would argue, and finally, we too realized that these distant apparitions could be people trying to cross the border in the dark. The Bund is a perfect east–west elevated walkway that can take you to your destination across the border. Those were the days when the borders were fenceless. Now, a strong chain link iron fence is there to stop the intruders.

The mound had remained a mysterious and unmapped feature, but for the limited surveys done during 1835 and 1846. Much of what we know about the landscape of Kutch comes from the descriptions by Sir Alexander Burnes[5] and W.E. Baker. Burnes was a British explorer and diplomat (of the same family as the poet Robert Burns) who wrote his travelogues of Afghanistan and Central Asia that relate experiences from the late 1820s to the late 1830s, including narrations of the 1819 earthquake. When Baker visited this area in 1844, the navigable channel had dried up. Although neither of these explorers travelled the entire length of the Bund, they made an initial estimate of 50 km, revised later to 80 km. Although erosion and tidal scouring were active between the earthquake and their visits, the overall topography of the Bund remains intact to this day. However, cross-cutting gullies have developed mainly in the western part.

The dramatic morphological features in the region, when read along with historical accounts of post-earthquake surveyors, reflect the changes the area has undergone. For example, Burnes refers to an important river passage through the Allah Bund as 'forty yards wide and about three fathoms deep in which the waters of the real Indus were passing to the oceans'.[6] This observation confirms that the river's course was re-established in the 1926 flood after being blocked during the 1819 uplift. On Burnes' subsequent visit in 1828, he found the flow had ceased. In 1844, during Baker's visit, the channel had dried up and was not navigable; consequently, the Bund was accessible only from the north and not from the Sindri Lake in the south. During our visit in 1999, we identified a 10 m wide and 3 m deep river valley towards the central part of the Bund. Location and morphological descriptions of the Bund conform to reports by Burnes. However, the width of the Bund appears to have been much reduced from what was initially described.

Sea Turning into Land

The biblical story goes like this: 'Then Moses stretched out his hand over the sea, and the Lord drove the sea back by a strong east wind all night and made the sea dry land, and the waters were divided.'[7] Scientists say it is impossible for the sea to part, exposing its floor, due to an agency like a strong wind. Be that as it may, coming back to the landscape of our interest, the Great Rann, evidence suggests that it was forced to rise above sea level to form the Rann of Kutch because of tectonic movements. A 1000-year-old map of the region available in various publications on the 1819 earthquake is a reminder that it used to be all sea but gradually transformed into the tidal flat of today. The 1819 earthquake and its equally potent predecessors contributed to its evolution by raising it from the depths.

The Rann of Kutch had been undersea when Alexander, the Macedonian king reached the western part of the Indian subcontinent. The history of this region has been well-documented for over 2000 years. For instance, some ancient scholars have referred to a disastrous sea-level variation in the Indus Delta and its consequences on the Macedonian fleet during Alexander's military campaign in 326/327 BCE. The proto-historical Harappan settlers in Dholavira, at the eastern extremity of the Rann, could have used the shallower sea at the time for trade about 4500 years ago. In the geographical notes written back in 1907 by Robert Sivewright,[8] the reader is apprised of how the Rann of Kutch was transformed from a shallow sea inlet to a tidal flat. Sindh was invaded by the Arabs in 712 CE, and the Arab chroniclers of the conquest furnish information on the delta's growth. After the Arab conquest of Sindh, the sea was still navigable for hundreds of years, though much shallower than it was during Alexander's time. The Rann had been gradually getting shallower and was raised due to vertical forces that precipitated the occasional large earthquakes, like the one in 1819.

Earthquakes of the Past

Based on historical reports from the bordering areas in Pakistan, there could have been several major or moderate earthquakes in the last 1000 years that impacted the ancient settlements. However, the dates and locations of these events remained unclear due to lack of reliable information. Archaeological excavations near the port city of Bhanbore attest that a significant earthquake occurred between 787 and 780 CE. The city was inhabited from the first century BCE to the thirteenth century CE. The 893 CE event reportedly destroyed the medieval port city of Bhanbore (also known as Daibul), and its fate was finally sealed by a massive flood on the Indus in 1226. Subsequently, the Indus River shifted its course, and the port had to be abandoned. Another historical city in the deltaic region of the Indus is the famous town of Mansurah about 200 km from Karachi, known as Brahmanabad before the Arab invasion. This ancient town was possibly destroyed in an earthquake in the tenth or eleventh century—a conclusion drawn from archaeological excavations. There are also reports of other earthquakes of indeterminate magnitude in 1668 and 1903 to the north-west of Bhanbore, possibly moderate in their intensities.[9]

Figure 6.4: The author near the ruins of the Vigakot Fort in 2019.

Our quest to trace the origins of any earthquake before the 1819 earthquake source has brought us to the fascinating Great Rann many times. The Survey of India maps identifies 'a fort in ruins' near Vigakot that was damaged in 1819. Bricks of the fort destroyed by the 1819 earthquake remain scattered around, reminiscent of a once-functional tax-collection centre. Red bricks cover an area of 500 sq. m on slightly elevated ground. Knowing how humans like to rebuild, we gathered this was a place to look for signs of any older constructions. A report on the 1819 earthquake[10] describes severe liquefaction that accompanied the earthquake that formed several sandblow craters. In the trenches excavated at the site of the ruins, we discovered fragments of bricks and traces of charcoal about 2 m below the surface.

It was clear that the ruins and the traditional kitchen were from an old settlement laid to waste by an older quake. When did that happen? Historical accounts depict Vigakot as an area of human settlement, including an active revenue outpost. Like the Sindri Fort in the downstream region, Vigakot could have been a fortified township. Similar sites along the waterways are now defunct due to landscape changes following the 1819 earthquake. Ancient settlements help generate reliable radiocarbon dates because of their organic remains. Excavations at this site exposed evidence for multiple liquefaction events, which cut through settlement horizons. We used pieces of charcoal from its ancient kitchen to date an earthquake between 885 and 1025 CE. This age falls in the same window as the earthquake of 800–1000 years by Roger Bilham and his co-worker Sarosh Lodi, near Mansurah, the eighth-century Arabic capital of the Sindh province, Pakistan.

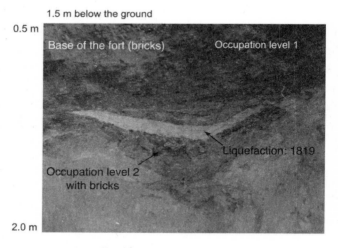

Figure 6.5: Wall of a trench excavated near Vigakot.

Mentioned in Hindu mythology as being episodically engulfed by the sea, Dwarka, an ancient city in north-western

Gujarat, could be another victim of past calamities. The onshore and offshore explorations revealed material that confirmed that Dwarka was occupied from the Protohistoric period (4000 years BCE). This site was likely struck by tsunamis in the past, originating from the Makran Sea to the west—a known source for tsunami earthquakes. That the Makran source remains active was brought to light by the event of 1945, which was reported along several locations along the west coast of India. Our excavations in Bet Dwarka, in collaboration with scientists from the National Institute of Oceanography (NIO), Goa, on an island 30 km north of Dwarka, suggested the disruption of an ancient cultural horizon about 2000 years ago. It is not clear if a nearby earthquake or a distant one caused this disruption. The 2001 Bhuj earthquake, discussed in the next chapter, is a reminder of the unknown earthquake sources in this region and their underestimated damage potential. Future earthquakes could be highly destructive because of rapid urbanization and high population density.

Chapter 7

The Rann Rumbles Again

I experienced the California Northridge Earthquake of 1994 and the eruption of Mount St. Helens in 1980, and I have thus seen first-hand how terrible and awesomely devastating a force of nature can be.

—*Paul Watson*

An opportunity to study two earthquakes in a row in the same region rarely happens in the lifetime of an earthquake scientist. We had been around in Kutch for nearly four years, since 1997, assessing the 1819 Allah Bund earthquake. We had completed the first phase of our work, and a significant research paper was in print in the *Bulletin of the Seismological Society of America*. We were excited about having mapped the morphology of the Indian part of Allah Bund from east to west, which Burnes and Baker had surveyed in part during their visits in the nineteenth century. With the new data, it was possible to explain its elevation and geometry. It is postulated that the massive liquefaction combined with tectonic subsidence due to the earthquake was possibly responsible for the flooding of Sindri Fort. But the earthquake of 1819 was not the end; a surprise awaited in the offing. The devil under the ground had returned.

A grave surprise came from another powerful earthquake that struck Gujarat on 26 January 2001. The most devastating earthquake in modern Indian history exposed the lack of preparedness and the vulnerability of poorly designed structures. The earthquake struck in the morning as India celebrated its 52nd Republic Day. Children had assembled in schools for celebrations; offices, shops and markets were closed. It was around 8.45 a.m. when the ground started shaking violently. This powerful earthquake killed over 20,000 people with an estimated loss of about Rs 22,000 crore, as per the EERI (Earthquake Engineering Research Institute, USA) surveys led by Sudhir Jain and a team from the Indian Institute of Technology, Kanpur.[1] The earthquake caused the failure of several earth dams, multi-storied reinforced concrete buildings and bridges. The strong shaking generated extensive liquefaction features in the entire region, as far as Hyderabad in Pakistan. Several craters exceeding 5 m in diameter and new streams also appeared at some locations. Sandblows were formed even in distant cities like Ahmedabad.

Many survivors narrated their heart-breaking experiences, but some are extraordinary, like Aakash[*] a native of Kutch and a theatre enthusiast, Aakash was part of a Kutchi film project. After a long day, he had wrapped up a segment on 25 January 2001 and gone to bed late in the evening. Like most youngsters, Aakash had read about earthquakes in books and newspapers but he had never experienced one. He helplessly watched as the few moments shattered the lives of many. The event changed his life and career. He decided to devote his future to assisting in disaster-affected areas. Currently working with the World Bank as a disaster risk management programme consultant,

---

[*] Name changed for privacy.

he is also a United Nations (UN) volunteer who works with NGOs dedicated to earthquake rehabilitation efforts.

Back in Kerala, relaxed and taking a day off from work, we were finishing our breakfast when television screens started airing news of the earthquake. Buildings collapsed like decks of cards; hundreds of people had died and communication lines were broken. Reports from various parts started pouring in. Our first thoughts were about friends living in Bhuj. Vigakot was far, and we reckoned that our friends at the BSF camp would be safe. With most telephone lines disrupted, there was no way of contacting anyone. After several attempts, we connected with our collaborator, Mahesh Thakkar, a young faculty member at the Lalan College of Bhuj (now the director of the Birbal Sahni Institute of Paleosciences). We caught him while he was still searching for his camera in the debris of his office that was severely damaged. Mahesh and his family, including his little daughter Antra, had survived. The apartment in which his mother was living was partially damaged, but she was safe. There was damage everywhere; fissures had developed on the ground and large ponds and water bodies had formed. We needed to start our work to understand the effects of the large earthquake. There was much to learn from the present to revisit the past.

On the Trail of the Bhuj Earthquake

The magnitude 7.7 earthquake originated in the village of Chobari, about 80 km east of Bhuj. The village, which was totally devastated by the earthquake, has now been rebuilt. The shattered homes were abandoned, but small shrines with saffron flags flying over them are built at these spots. Lamps are lit at these spots every day to keep the memories of the villagers' loved ones alive.

Bhuj was in ruins, and so was the nearby town of Anjar. Many distant cities were also affected, most significantly the city of Ahmedabad, about 250 km from the epicentre. Several multi-storeyed buildings collapsed here. This kind of response to a distant earthquake was unexpected, but geotechnical engineers gave an explanation.[2] The city of Ahmedabad is situated on the banks of the Sabarmati River, where the alluvial deposits amplify seismic energy and cause liquefaction. Both these phenomena affect the buildings. Not surprising that the compromised engineering designs of the multi-storeyed buildings contributed to structural failure. Several studies that followed confirmed this view and attributed site amplification of seismic waves by soft sediments to explain the severity of the damage.

The 2001 earthquake was comparable to the 1819 earthquake in its energy release, but surprisingly, it had no primary surface fault. Seismologists modelled the source using instrumentally recorded data and found the blind fault and the earthquake's focus at a depth of about 25 km. Seismologists also used the data to infer the direction of the stress that operates in the region, and as expected, it was roughly in the north-east direction and was consistent with the direction of India–Eurasia plate convergence. It is considered as 'expected' because regions away from the plate boundaries are also influenced by the stresses originating there and are sufficient to trigger earthquakes on pre-existing faults. In the Kutch region, the pre-existing faults were created during the formation of the Kutch rift. The rifting occurred during the Jurassic to the early Cretaceous Period (170 to 66 million years ago) but stopped after the collision of the India–Eurasia plates. However, the large faults created during the rifting has left the original structures dormant that have the potential to be reactivated.

Although there are many mapped faults in the region, the earthquake was not spatially associated with any of them. There was not any primary surface rupture or topographic surface expression, as in the case of its 1819 predecessor. Geologists call such hidden faults 'blind' because their expressions do not reach the surface. There were no immediate aftershocks shallower than 10 km, which was another indication that the fault may not have reached the surface. Blind faults create subtle evidence of ground deformation, often in the form of folding of the top layers, which are not easily recognized. A well-trained field geologist in our team picked a gentle fold in a cultivated field where plants along a 50 m stretch had dried up as folding had raised them above the irrigated soil.

The trenches we excavated near the Vigakot craters exposed two older sandblows from the 1819 earthquake and its nearly 1000-year-old predecessor. Our studies also led to the identification of an earthquake that affected this region about 4000 years ago. However, a period during which no significant earthquake seems to have passed, as is evident from archaeological records. For example, the fort in Dholavira, a site of the Harappan settlement, had reportedly sustained partial damage attributable to a distant earthquake between 4000 and 4500 years ago and had undergone restoration. There was no further record of earthquake-related damage to this structure. The 2001 earthquake also did not create any damage except knocking down a few bricks. Our excavations in the areas affected by the 2001 earthquake exposed evidence of an older earthquake about 3500–4000 years ago, but this date is not well-constrained. The Kutch region has a history of earthquakes originating from multiple independent sources, and the 1819 or 2001 events are only the most recent ones with different sources.

Interplate, Intraplate or Moot

When Arch Johnston, who was heading the CERI (Centre for Earthquake Research and Information) in Memphis (USA) informed us that he would land in Bhuj after the earthquake, we were excited. His 1982 paper on New Madrid seismicity published in *Scientific American*[3] was quite popular not just among scientists but also among non-experts due to the importance of the topic. His articles on the earthquakes in the continental (plate) interiors profoundly influenced us. He was particularly curious about the Kutch earthquakes because of the similarity of the region with the 1811–12 earthquakes of New Madrid. It was not easy to explain this sequence of earthquakes of 7.5–8 in the middle of a continent where stress build-up is minuscule. In the plate tectonics paradigm, the relative motion of the interacting plates provides enough fuel to produce earthquakes, but such a refuelling does not happen away from the zone plate interactions. So, what keeps the faults within the continental interiors 'rockin' and rollin'' is a question that makes the seismologists scratch their heads. Several recent works have been able to unravel the mysteries of the New Madrid earthquakes.

Arch Johnston and his colleague Paul Bodin who visited Kutch, were struck by the Bhuj earthquake's similarities with the 1811–12 New Madrid earthquakes, such as its association with an ancient rift, its magnitude and its lack of surface rupture. Both the 1819 and 2001 events have evoked much academic interest worldwide because they are located far from plate boundaries.

*Figure 7.1: A sandblow near Vigakot formed
by the 2001 earthquake.*

The sources of the earthquakes of 1811–12 are located
more than a thousand kilometres from the plate boundary.
Relatively away from the plate boundary, the Indian
earthquakes in 1819 and 2001 are arguably classified as
SCR earthquakes and most often compared to the plate
interior earthquakes of the United States, like the 1810–11
New Madrid and 1886 Charleston earthquakes. The 2001
event led to an intense debate among the seismologists
concerning whether the Kutch region was part of a
diffuse plate boundary. The title of one of the abstracts
of a paper submitted to the American Geophysical Union
in December 2001 reflects this raging controversy: 'The
2001 Bhuj earthquake: Interplate, Intraplate or Moot.'[4]
Investigations following the 2001 earthquake studies also
found that the sources of the 1819 and 2001 earthquakes
are not similar in their productivity. The northern side of
the Kutch region, related to the 1819 source, appears to

be more productive, with earthquakes occurring in about 1000 years. With no detectable events during the last 4000 years, earthquakes on the southern side which hosted the 2001 event seem to have a longer recurrence period.[5]

* * *

Chapter 8

The Rocking North-East

It is the nature of the earth to shift. It is the nature of fragile things to break. It is the nature of fire to burn.
—*Susan Meissner,* The Nature of Fragile Things

Bordered by the Himalayas, the most active continental collision boundary in the world along its northern margin and an active subduction zone along its eastern margin, the Indian plate is unique. As the Indian plate moves eastward and dives beneath the Burmese plate, it forms the Indo-Burman mountain ranges. This mountain range extends further south to join the Andaman–Nicobar Islands where the Indian Oceanic plate plunges beneath the continental Eurasian Plate and forms a subduction zone. The north-eastern part of India's plate boundary consists of seven states, referred to as 'the seven sisters'—Arunachal Pradesh, Assam, Manipur, Meghalaya, Mizoram, Nagaland and Tripura. Much of the region remains unexplored, owing to the formidable terrain marked by rugged mountain ranges, hills, rainforests, rivers and jungles. This part of India, constituting about 8 per cent of the country's geographical area, boasts of the highest biodiversity density found anywhere in the world. With its picturesque mountains, hills, valleys, vegetation and various life forms, this geographic region is endowed with natural beauty. Much of the north-eastern region falls in one of Earth's most seismically active regions, making it an important entry in this book.

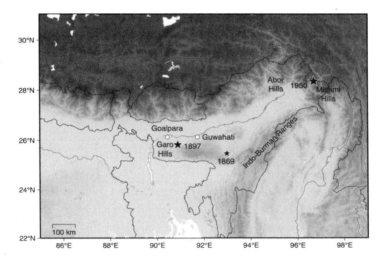

Figure 8.1: Map of north-east India showing locations of large earthquakes.

The active tectonic movements along the eastern and north-eastern collision boundaries have given rise to many spectacular mountain ranges and river systems that have shaped this unusual landscape. Here, the mighty Brahmaputra River, known as the Yarlung Tsangpo in China, cuts through the Himalayan gorges into Arunachal Pradesh and flows south-west through the Assam Valley, crossing international borders between India, China and Bangladesh. With its enormous natural resources, the Brahmaputra River and its tributaries form the 'lifeline' for large communities in north-eastern India. As one of the world's river basins impacted by anthropogenic activities, the Brahmaputra River basin faces threats from floods and other environmental hazards.

As we read in the chapter on plate tectonics, the boundaries between two tectonic plates are the sources of great inter-plate earthquakes. While most inter-plate earthquakes occur along the boundaries of continental-Oceanic plates (Japanese earthquakes, for example), the Himalayas form the most active inter-plate boundary between two continental plates. With a magnitude 8.7, the largest documented continental inter-plate earthquake history occurred in north-east India on 15 August 1950. North-east India was also the source of another great earthquake in 1897, located on the northern fringe of the Shillong plateau. Although the Shillong plateau is not exactly on the plate boundary, many researchers believe that the outlying regions of a plate boundary are also influenced by similar tectonic stresses and hence seismically productive. Following this concept, Kailash Khattri, former professor at the University of Roorkee (now IIT), suggested that a seismic gap existed between the 1987 Shillong and 1950 Assam earthquakes, like the Central Gap in the eastern part of the Himalayas.[1]

Historical records testify that earthquakes were not new to the people of Shillong; they often experienced mild tremors. Especially after the large magnitude 7.4 earthquake of 1869 near Cachar, about 200 km south-east of Shillong, several aftershocks had been rocking the region. In 1875, another light to moderate quake jolted Shillong. Maybe because of these occasional shocks, many residents in Shillong had developed an intuitive feeling of an impending major one. The massively destructive earthquake that jolted the Shillong plateau in 1897 brought down buildings, bridges and houses to a heap of rubble. Though its centre was Shillong, its effect extended to distant Calcutta and Bhagalpur with record-breaking high intensity. Initially, the magnitude was estimated to be 8.7 and was later revised as ~8.2; the earthquake occurred at 5.11 p.m., Saturday, 12 June.

One of India's endearing storytellers, Ruskin Bond, wrote an earthquake story on the background of the 1897 event. Bond was not born then, and the account had been passed down by his father, a child living with his parents in Shillong at that time. Bond has narrated how his grandfather was in the habit of spending long hours in his bathtub, splashing water, singing to himself and sometimes falling asleep in it. Once, he was in his bath when a cyclone blew away the roof of the house. A joke and concern in the family was if a natural calamity like an earthquake occurred, his grandfather could be trapped in the bathroom. Worried about her husband's bathing habit, his grandmother always kept watch on him. Bond narrates that his grandfather was in the bathtub when the earthquake finally occurred. But this time, he surprised everyone with the alacrity to jump out and escape to safety through a less obstructive back door of his house to join the rest of the family.[2]

Eyewitness Reports

Many British officers in colonial India habitually made notes on natural disasters, and quite a few were in the form of letters to their family members or colleagues. We have much first-hand information about this earthquake from the letters of Thomas Henry Digges La Touche (1856–1938), a geologist at the Geological Survey of India. Designated to report the effect of the earthquake, La Touche prepared detailed descriptions. He made meticulous notes of his daily observations, some of which were transmitted to his wife through his daily letters. Transcriptions of his letters and handwritten notes are preserved at the British Library and the Centre of South Asian Studies, Cambridge University. In his letter from Calcutta on 14 June 1897, he comments about the damage: 'The damage done is enormous. A great many houses ought to be rebuilt entirely but the native owners will probably only patch them up till the next big earthquake comes and then they will collapse entirely.' These letters, compiled and published in 2018 by the American seismologist Roger Bilham,[3] vividly describe the earthquake scenes.

Figure 8.2: The collapsed bridge near Shillong.

The letter of 29 June 1897 that May Sweet, wife of a British official named Williamson Sweet, wrote to her sister Mrs Godfrey is another vivid eyewitness account of the earthquake.

At 5.30 on Saturday last, the 12th June was as usual, and 30 seconds afterwards was completely in ruins. I was riding on the Gauhati Road with Mr. Monaghan, and suddenly we heard a queer rumbling sound and then trees swayed every way. Luckily by instinct we both turned sharply to the left and galloped up the hill as far as we could find a place. We had crossed the bridge which would have gone down under us. I can't possibly describe the sensation as it was so totally different from anything I had ever experienced. I did not know whether I was on my horse on the land or in the air. I could do nothing as the ground was all in a whirl. I know I looked once at Mr M., and he was as pale as death.[4]

Figure 8.3: A sandblow formed during the 1897 earthquake.

A Reverend's Description Turned Spiritual

Reverend Robert Evans of the Welsh Calvinistic Methodist Presbyterian Mission has vividly documented the 1897 earthquake. Reverend Evans was engaged in humanitarian relief work for victims in the Khasi Hills at the time. His eyewitness account, which was lying for a long time in the Dylan Thomas Centre, National Library in Aberystwyth, Wales, was published by the Indian History Congress (2004).[5] Here we reproduce his writings in part:

The very face of the land underwent huge changes. At the end of that short spell, every stone house had become a pile of rubble, while every wooden house was bent and twisted, taking on almost every shape imaginable, until they were totally unsuitable for habitation. Massive landslips took place in every direction. In some places, hundreds of thousands of tons of earth from the hill slopes were carried down many hundreds of feet with a deafening thud. Within a few seconds, lofty hillsides, previously made beautiful by grass and trees, were visibly denuded in every part, the biggest ones looked like huge quarries, while those in the distance resembled ploughed land. Great floors were hurled to the valley floors and so were the earth and rocks from under them, until the land was made to appear raw red and scarred, whereas, earlier, it looked smooth and verdant. All the roads and paths on the slopes were ripped away so that getting from one place to another became impossible.

He continues with a spiritual undertone:

The earth resembled a child having convulsions. For a minute or so, the assault went on in every direction with unstoppable force, then it calmed down for about the same length of time. Every commotion caused the earth to rage like a wounded beast in dire agony—or, more as if all the beasts of the earth were groaning together. That was our plight when the evening shadows began to spread across the land. It is not easy to describe the feelings of those who spent that night amid the roaring and the tremors, the rain and the dark. A night never to be forgotten! Everyone awaited the morning far more eagerly than the night watchman did. Without a doubt, that was the most drawn-out, anxious and comfortless night we had ever spent. And oh! How good it was to see the light of day! . . . In the morning light, the scenes that met our eyes were really weird—destruction of every kind on all sides. The blue-green slopes had been converted into scarred bare rock. The face of the land had changed beyond belief, inasmuch as some hills had gone down considerably while others had risen . . .

The 1897 Shillong Earthquake: Beginning of the Modern Seismology

What La Touche, May Sweet and Robert Evans have narrated in their letters are eyewitness accounts of one of the most significant nineteenth-century earthquakes. As the largest earthquake to occur when modern seismographs had just come into broader use, it attracted global attention. It was the largest instrumentally recorded earthquake for which seismic records were available and unsurprisingly, it opened new vistas in observational seismology. The monograph by R.D. Oldham, who was working with the Geological Survey of India at a time is regarded as a classic field report of an earthquake that is followed by students of seismology. Oldham's report[6] published in 1899 describes the destruction and ground failures and provides information on ground accelerations, which exceeded the Earth's gravitational acceleration. Based on Oldham's report, the earthquake caused maximum destruction in Shillong and Guwahati, where most government buildings were located. It is reported to have destroyed most buildings and almost all stonework in and around Shillong, including many bridges, stone houses and churches. Oldham reported that places near Shillong plateau observed the maximum intensity.

The earthquake triggered landslides from the Garo Hills and other distant locations. Guwahati and Goalpara, which border the Brahmaputra River, experienced warping, tilting and intense ground motion. The Brahmaputra floodplain and the neighbouring areas were particularly vulnerable to soil liquefaction due to the prolonged vibration of the ground, where the water-saturated loose sediment is highly susceptible to liquefaction. Severe coseismic liquefaction led to sand venting in areas far beyond the plateau margins, and that created fissures and sandblows over a wide area of Lower Assam, Meghalaya, West Bengal and northern Bangladesh.

Figure 8.4: A transient lake that formed after the 1897 earthquake.

The isoseismal map[*] prepared by Oldham had the shape of a hat. The peculiar shape of the high-intensity zone was attributed to the selective amplification in the Brahmaputra valley. Analysis of data from the 1897 earthquake led to many important observations and developments in seismology. Oldham used instrumental records to provide the first clear evidence for P, S and surface waves, an observation that forms the backbone of modern seismological research. He noted that the seismometers located on the opposite side

---

[*] An isoseismal is a contour or line on a map connecting points of equal intensity relating to a specific earthquake and confining the area within which the intensity is the same. An isoseismal map provides a measure of the size of the areas over which an earthquake was felt at different intensities. It is an indirect measure of the energy released by the event. It is not instrumentally measured, but inferred from ground observations of the way people felt the earthquake and how budlings responded to the ground shaking.

of the Earth from the earthquake detected P-waves later than expected. Further, there was an area of the earth from angular distances of 104 to 140 degrees (shadow zone) that did not receive any direct P-waves.

From the subdued S-wave and the presence of the shadow zone, he concluded that the Earth must have a central core through which P-waves travel with a substantially lower velocity than the surrounding material. The magnitude of the event was calculated using the instrumentally recorded data independently by two pioneering seismologists, Beno Gutenberg and Charles Richter, two names that keep cropping up in this book.

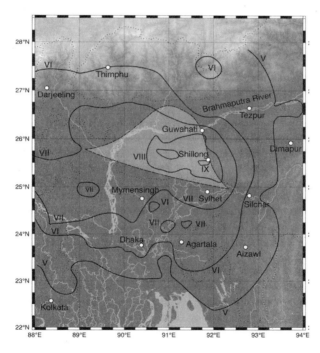

Figure 8.5: Intensity map of the 1897 earthquake.

Historical Earthquakes in Assam

Historical records on Assam are quite informative about its
ancient temples, some of which have existed for more than
1500 years. Their documented restoration and reconstruction
history bears testimony to the ground-shaking effects of great
earthquakes that must have impacted this region. References
to earthquake-related damage found in ancient books such
as the Kalika Purana and Yogini Tantra (late ninth and
sixteenth century CE.) suggest that a wave of reconstruction
activity occurred in many parts of the state around 850 CE,
but it is unclear whether this was after any earthquake. It is
common knowledge that people seldom abandon temples.
Even when they are partially or fully destroyed, they are
invariably reconstructed, often salvaging what has survived.
For example, take the case of the sixth century CE temple
located at Da-Parbatia near Tezpur. The circa eighteenth-
century CE structure collapsed during the 1897 earthquake
and exposed a stone door frame dating back to the fifth to
sixth century CE. The coexistence of these structures, which
follow distinctly different styles of construction, suggested
multiple episodes of destruction, and in this case, the
earthquake occurred after the sixth century.

The ancient books also refer to the destruction of the
temple of Kamakhya (seventh to eighth century CE) on
the top of Nilachal Hills, about 8 km from the town of
Guwahati. Our excavations near the Kamakhya temple
revealed destruction at two levels—from the 1897
earthquake and an older one. The age of pottery found at
the level of destruction combined with geological evidence
suggests that the earthquake could be 1200 years old
(with some margin for error). This could be the destructive
eighth-century event described in the Kalika Purana and
Yogini Tantra.[7]

Ancient structures with documented histories also serve as good historical seismographs. The ancient Sil-sáko bridge built over the Barnadi River is a good example to calibrate the record of destructive earthquakes that have affected the region. A description of this bridge across the Barnadi (at present a dry channel) is available in the notes made in 1851 by Major S.T. Hannay, commander of the First Assam Light Infantry. He noted that the design and style of architecture of this bridge are coeval with that of the ancient stone temples built during a long period from the fifth to tenth century CE. Going by his report, the 42 m long stone bridge existed sometime during the fifth to the eleventh century CE and was used in 1205 CE by an invading cavalry to reach Bhutan.[8] It retained its integrity until 1851 but collapsed during the 1897 earthquake. As the long-standing bridge survived until the 1897 earthquake, it would appear that during the intervening period of 692 years (1205–1897), the region did not experience a similarly large earthquake. But this matter is subject to interpretation as the region was not entirely earthquake-free. For instance, indigenous Assamese works mention a 'violent' earthquake in 1548 CE and describe how pebbles and sand water came out bursting the surface. These descriptions are available in the ancient chronicles of the late medieval Ahom kingdom known as Buranji (written in the Ahom language). Another event of some consequence occurred in 1663 CE.[9] Information about these earthquakes is mainly in the form of descriptions whose interpretations vary, so their locations are not certain.

Where Is the Fault?

Today seismologists and engineers require detailed information such as dimensions of the fault, nature of displacement (vertical, horizontal, etc.), depth where earthquake originated and the ground conditions to make assessments about the regional seismic hazard. Quite often this information may not be available. For example, the fault itself may not be exposed on the surface, limiting further details on its dimensions. The lack of a surface expression from the great Shillong earthquake has remained a topic of discussion. Although Oldham's monograph had established the status of the 1897 earthquake as the best documented among the nineteenth-century events, the causative fault was unclear. Oldham initially believed that the earthquake was caused by a fault below the plateau at a depth ranging from 8–14 km, but in the absence of a recognizable primary rupture, this could not be confirmed. Another question is whether the earthquake had occurred on the Himalayan plate boundary or on any independent fault system. The scenic southern border of the plateau defined by the Dauki fault was also considered a potential source.

The 1897 earthquake is one of the rare events for which pre- and post-event triangulation survey data are available. More than 100 years after the earthquake, Roger Bilham and Philip England used the data on land-level changes to identify the fault that caused the 1897 earthquake. Their models, published in 2001 in the journal *Nature*, suggested that the earthquake was caused by a south-dipping structure and that it was not a plate boundary event. Later research published in 2015 in the journal *Tectonics* by the same researchers reiterates their previous conclusion that the fault ruptured close to the northern edge of the Shillong plateau.[10]

The 1950 Earthquake—The Largest Continental Event

Popularly known as the Assam earthquake (and as Chayu or Medog earthquake), the 1950 event originated in the rugged mountainous areas between the Himalayas and the

Hengudan mountain range (south-west China). Felt over 3 million sq. km in India, Myanmar (Burma), Bangladesh (then East Pakistan), Tibet and southern China, the earthquake caused extensive damage in many towns of Upper Assam and regions across the eastern Himalayas. It also affected Abor and Mishmi Hills and most of the Assam plains. When the earthquake occurred Kingdon-Ward, an English botanist and explorer, was camping in Rima, a tiny hamlet on the slopes of the eastern Himalayas, near the Tibetan–Burmese border. He heard heavy explosive sounds following the shock, coming apparently from high in the air.[11] While at Rima. Ward witnessed violent shaking, extensive slides and the rise of the streams. Slices of the hills had slid down, transforming the Brahmaputra River into an endless expanse of water. The earthquake severely damaged the forest along the banks of the river and the foothills. He heard heavy explosive sounds following the shock, coming from high in the air; such sounds were heard at many points in India and Burma, as far as 1200 km from the source of the earthquake. Although Ward was stationed near the quake's source, he had little opportunity to make detailed observations. His primary concern was getting out of the turmoil and finding a way to head back to India.

15 August 1950 was an auspicious day, the third year of India's Independence. People all over India were celebrating, and the nation's mood was upbeat. In the widely tribal Assam Valley in the country's north-eastern corner surrounded by the Himalayan mountains, it was already dark by 7.30 p.m., and the jubilant crowd was concluding the celebrations and getting ready to retire for the day. This was when they felt the earth tremble. Described as the home of earthquakes, the people of Assam have experienced many shocks, but none were as big.

The shaking lasted four minutes and was so strong that slices of land moved, causing massive landslides and producing vast loads of debris choking the rivers. The epicentral region comprised the Abhor and Mishmi Hills in Arunachal Pradesh. E.P. Gee, a naturalist and a tea planter who had spent long years in Assam, noted that it was of greater intensity than the severe earthquakes of 1897 (Shillong), 1934 (Bihar) and 1935 (Quetta). He quotes some friends about their earthquake experiences: 'The earth heaved and rolled with sickly undulating movement. Cars parked on level surfaces with brakes unapplied careered wildly about, fans swung, and some lights went out . . . In the end, there was a succession of loud booming noises described as resembling anti-aircraft fire.'[12] The Geological Survey of India assigned the task of collecting information about the effects of the earthquake to M.C. Poddar. At a time when the theory of plate tectonics had not taken shape, scientists, including him, were challenged to explain the earthquake's cause. Poddar's report gives details of ground deformation and occurrence of liquefaction during the earthquake.[13]

The earthquake did not originate strictly within the Indian territory but near Rima. However, it was more damaging in Assam. Recollections by Renu Majumdar, interviewed by Angana Majumdar and published by *The Sentinel*, Assam's English daily newspaper, give a rare insight from the first-person experience of this great earthquake. Renu was fifteen years old at the time of the earthquake and she describes the event as '. . . a strong tremor and a loud sound in the evening. The house started trembling suddenly, and the ground started shaking violently . . .' She recalled how the tall coconut trees got buried so deep at a place known as Sadiya that the people could directly pluck the fruits from the ground.[14] Her vivid description shows the voluminous amount of sediment and debris that might have accumulated over the surface to sink a coconut tree, even a young one with a moderate height of a few metres. These sediments must have eventually reached the delta front of the Bangladesh plains and helped the islands grow faster.

Some newspapers reported that volcanic activity was the cause of the earthquake. Poddar had figured out that earthquakes related to volcanism would typically be associated with many localized tremors, and the activity would decrease rapidly. As this was not the case, he ruled out volcanism and proposed a 'tectonic origin' on faults along the India–China border. Indeed, a remarkable proposition, nearly two decades before plate tectonic theory found wider acceptance. In his reports based on post-earthquake surveys, Poddar reported extensive damage to many towns of upper Assam, with about 1500 casualties on the Indian side. Most likely, an equal number or more had died in the hilly terrain on the Chinese and the Burmese side. The highest felt intensities were reported from a narrow quadrant to the south-west, possibly because of the amplification of shaking effects within the alluvium. The instrumentally recorded magnitude of the earthquake was 8.7. The aftershocks lasted for about eight months, and many of them were above magnitude 6. The data collected by A.N. Tandon, the noted Indian seismologist, was used to estimate the geographical spread of the aftershock and epicentre of the great earthquake. From such data, the Indian Seismological Service established an enormous geographical reach of this activity, extending to the source region of a 7.3 magnitude earthquake near Tibet, which occurred in 1947. If indeed this was a foreshock remains a tantalizing question, but in the absence of authentic data this question remains unanswered.

Apart from causing damage to property, the earthquake also impacted communication systems. Rail communications in the region had to be suspended due to damage to the tracks and bridges. The *Times of India* of 21 November 1950 reported a staggering number of 12,000 buildings and 2000 granaries destroyed.[15] In the land known for its sprawling tea plantations spread over 342 acres, the earthquake destroyed nearly 126 acres. Shaking effects were compounded by the flood and the rivers, bringing down sand, mud, trees and debris because of the monsoon. Pilots flying over the affected areas reported significant changes in topography and the destruction of forests, mainly due to enormous landslides and debris flow. Many hills were sheared, and the rock debris fell into the valleys below, blocking and breaching the rivers and generating flash floods downstream. The earthquake-induced landslides, floods and erosion of the riverbanks impacted forests and destroyed wildlife. On the Indian side, more than 1500 people lost their lives. The loss of cattle is estimated to be from 50,000 to 1,00,000.

In the Assam Valley, the river flows connect people and places and sustain the economy and social life. The earthquake could have mobilized about 47 cubic km of material, resulting in a high sediment load in the Brahmaputra. It took many years to flush the sediment through its lower courses. The abnormal river pattern continued for several years since the earthquake, affecting the lives of local communities in myriad ways. There was a depletion of river-borne fish due to increased mud and depletion in the oxygen level. In summary, the 1950 earthquake caused a long-lasting disruption to social and economic activities like no other earthquake, including the one in 1897. Some lakes formed by temporary damming endured for a long time as a reminder of how earthquake changes the landscape permanently. The Shonga-tser Lake, created after the earthquake, is a great tourist attraction today due to its scenic beauty. After the Bollywood movie *Koyla* was shot here, the lake was named 'Madhuri Lake' after Madhuri Dixit, one of India's legendary actors. No doubt, the lake is quite a breathtaking sight. This scenic splendour reminds the visitors of earthquakes' role in sustaining the natural world—whether in raising the mountains or forming the lakes—where life thrives despite the destruction to built environments.

Figure 8.6: Madhuri (Shonga-tser) Lake.

* * *

The Tectonically Active North-East India

The collision boundary formed by the central Himalayan arc runs in the west-north-west to east-south-east direction for about 2400 km. The relatively simpler and arcuate structure along its central segment is an expression of the subduction of the Indian plate beneath the Eurasia plate. The opposite ends of the Himalaya arc are marked by the western and eastern syntaxes, which occur as sharp bends. The eastern Himalayan syntaxis, considered the source of the great 1950 Assam earthquake, is structurally complex. Three major tectonic plates—India, Eurasia and Sunda—converge here, leading to its structural complexity.

The region represented as north-eastern India has undergone various phases of tectonism ever since it broke away from the Gondwanaland about 250 million years ago. The last phase of tectonism commenced with its collision with Myanmar in the east and Tibet in the north about 50 million years back. The collision, which has given rise to the eastern Indo-Burmese ranges, is continuing. After India's collision with Asia, the convergence rate between southern Tibet and India slowed down, to an estimated at 18 mm/year (estimate from eastern Nepal). Along the eastern boundary, the convergence rate is 17 mm/year. The active tectonic movements along the eastern and north-eastern collision boundaries have given rise to many spectacular mountain ranges and river systems that have shaped this unusual landscape.

The complexity and faster convergence make the north-eastern margin of the Indian subcontinent seismically productive. The landscape of north-east India is dominated mostly by the alluvial plains of the Brahmaputra River. To its south lies the Shillong plateau with its peak at about 2000 m above the mean sea level.

Chapter 9

Events Defining a Gap

Everything suddenly started shaking. It wasn't too severe at first and we all managed to get out of the building, then when we were in the yard outside everything started shaking very strongly and we were all bending down on the ground to stop from falling over and keeping as far away from the walls as possible.

*—An eyewitness account of the
2015 Nepal earthquake*

In 2001, a paper in the journal *Science* postulated that one or more great earthquakes are overdue in a large segment of the Himalayas.[1] The team of authors that included the foremost seismologists Roger Bilham, Vinod Gaur and Peter Molnar, cautioned that the damage from such an earthquake would be unparalleled. The population of India has more than doubled since the last great Assam Himalaya earthquake in 1950. The urban population in the Gangetic plain has increased by a factor of ten since the 1905 Kangra earthquake, and the ensuing risk from a modern-day earthquake would be manifold. Since the publication of the paper in 2001, the risk of an impending Himalayan earthquake has been an active topic of discussion among scientists, the media and the public.

Two events set the backdrop of this story—the 1905 Kangra (M_w 7.8) and the 1934 Bihar–Nepal (M_w 8.3) earthquakes. The unbroken patch of the Himalayan plate boundary between these two earthquakes, identified as the central seismic gap, is the unpredictable villain of the piece (see Figure 2.2 to locate the gap).

Three massive earthquakes (Kangra, 1905; Nepal-Bihar, 1934; Upper Assam, 1950) have occurred along the Himalayan plate boundary during the last century. Historical reports mention the earthquakes of 1803 CE (Garhwal Himalaya)[2] and 1833 CE (Central Nepal). Medieval chronicles refer to older earthquakes (1255, 1344 and 1505 CE).[3] Based on historical and archaeological evidence, an earthquake strong enough to level the temples in Garhwal and Kumaun has not occurred since the fifteenth century. However, the results of geological excavations in the region by various teams, including Senthil Kumar, Steve Wesnousky and others. published in 2010, have presented evidence of a great earthquake between the thirteenth and fifteenth centuries.[4] The premise is that the 700 km long segment between the 1905 and the 1934 earthquakes has not produced any great earthquake in the last 500 years. Considering the long-elapsed time since the previous earthquake, seismologists consider it a smoking gun, capable of hosting a large or great earthquake. Experiences of the two previous earthquakes and the developmental activities that have occurred since then make the projection of a future earthquake scenario quite grim.

The 1905 Earthquake that Shook the Kangra Valley

'He, who holds the Kangra Fort, holds the hills' is a popular saying among the hill people that goes well with the longevity and strength of the Kangra Fort in Himachal Pradesh. Located 20 km away from the town of Dharamshala, this is the oldest fort in India. It is believed to have been constructed by the royal family of Kangra around the fourth century BCE. The fort has witnessed the rise and fall of many kings and dynasties—Greeks, the kings of Kashmir, Afghans, Tughlaqs, Mughals and the British. In all these turbulent times, it stood like a mountain that did not move until the 1905 Kangra earthquake shook its foundations.

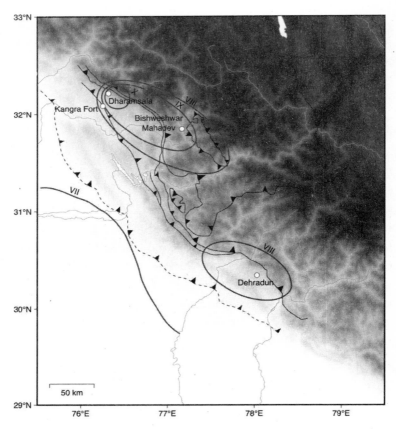

Figure 9.1: Location of the 1905 Kangra earthquake and the isoseismal (based on Middlemiss, 1905).

The 1905 Kangra earthquake occurred in a region surrounding two landmark towns, Kangra and Dharamshala. The extensive surveys conducted by Charles Middlemiss of the Geological Survey of India have given complete details of the effects of the earthquake. He reported, '. . . not a single railway has recorded any damage to the track, not a single road or path has been deflected, raised or lowered, no rivers or streams have changed their courses or been temporarily dammed up—except as due directly to landslides from slopes of such steepness that they might as easily have occurred after a heavy torrential rain-storm'.[5] The earthquake killed over 20,000 people in the Kangra valley and destroyed nearly 1,00,000 dwellings.[6] It registered the highest number of casualties and unprecedented extent of damage among the twentieth-century earthquakes in India. Landslides and rockfalls blocked the roads. Although most destroyed buildings were in Kangra and Dharamshala, many large cities in Punjab's plains also reported damages. The earthquake was felt over much of the northern subcontinent, as far east as Kolkata.

The highest intensity isoseismals were distributed within the Dharamsala-Kangra-Kullu area. An isolated patch of Rossi Forrel intensity VIII near Dehradun, ~250 km south-east of the epicentre, was an intriguing aspect of this earthquake. The additional patch of high intensity, located away from the epicentre of the earthquake, was identified by Middlemiss during the post-earthquake surveys. It was interpreted variously as a large aftershock or site amplification due to local soil conditions. The debate continued until a team of earthquake scientists led by Susan Hough of the US Geological Survey revisited the Kangra earthquake 100 years later and recalibrated some of its critical parameters. They reported that the rupture length of the fault is not more than 110 km, consistent with the revised magnitude of 7.8. The isolated patch of Rossi Forrel intensity VIII near Dehradun, ~250 km south-east of the epicentre, interpreted previously as an aftershock or as the result of local site amplification, was also revisited by them. Using global seismic records from Germany, they interpreted the high-intensity patch at Dehradun as an effect of the Moho reflection[*] and not an independent shock.

Figure 9.2: Barjeshwari Devi Temple, Kangra, after the earthquake.

---

[*] The Moho, defined as the boundary between the Earth's crust and the underlying upper mantle, occurs at depths of about 5–7 km beneath the oceans and 30–40 km below continents. Because of the variations of physical properties, such as density, across this boundary, parts of the incident seismic waves are reflected and rest is transmitted. This process is called the Moho reflection. The travel time of the reflected waves provide an estimate of the depth to the Moho.

Is the Kangra Valley Sleeping?

An important question is if any other large earthquake has shaken the Kangra region in the past few centuries. The 1905 earthquake is the largest in recent history in the Kangra region and there is no information on previous large historical earthquakes. But the region was not exactly quiet seismically. A few earthquakes, although not comparable to the 1905 event, have occurred elsewhere in Himachal Pradesh. The 19 January 1975 Kinnaur earthquake with a magnitude of 6.7, killed sixty people,[7] and the 1986 Dharamshala earthquake of magnitude 5.7, that killed six people are notable among them. The state has witnessed several other moderate and small events.

What about periods prior to instrumental recording? To develop a history of earthquakes in the region one has to go through the archives of history and archaeology. This would require finding evidence of destruction caused by ground shaking, which can be discriminated from vandalism. The Kullu Valley, considered the abode of gods and goddesses, has several temples with unique architecture, some more than 1000 years old. By a careful scrutiny of the history of such long-standing structures, information about destruction from ground shaking can be deciphered. Basheswar Mahadev Temple, located in Bajaura village near Kullu, is one such structure.

Figure 9.3: Basheswar Mahadev Temple at Bajaura.

The ninth-century Basheswar Mahadev Temple built
on the banks of the Beas River, the largest temple in the
Kullu region, is famous for its religious significance and
architectural splendour. Possibly due to the amazing
architecture of this stone temple, it is resistant to shaking
and the 1905 earthquake did not damage it. During his
post-earthquake surveys, Middlemiss had visited this site.
He did not observe any damage to the temple from the
1905 earthquake, but noticed lateral offsets in several
blocks of the structure. Such lateral offsets are known to

occur from ground motions during an earthquake, and not by vandalism. Thus he concluded that the region must have been affected by earthquakes in the past. So, did another earthquake affect the temple, but not the older Kangra Fort? Or is it the structural integrity of the Fort that left it intact? Geologic investigations in the area have not led to any clear evidence for past earthquakes in the area. But one thing is quite clear. Earthquakes have occurred in the Kangra area before 1905, and they will occur again, as the India-Eurasia plate continues to converge.

An Event that Shook the Plains: The Great 1934 Earthquake

'On Monday, the 15th January, at about 14h 14 m Calcutta experienced an earthquake shock of fair intensity which lasted for over three minutes. Buildings swayed, free-hanging objects oscillated vigorously, and even persons in motion were affected.'[8] These are the opening remarks of a paper published in March 1934 in *Current Science* by M.S. Krishnan of the Geological Survey of India. The devastating M_w 8.4 quake originated about 10 km south of Mt Everest. The ground movement lasted about five minutes in the central tract of Bihar; almost the whole of northern and central India perceived the shock. In Nepal and India, countless houses and invaluable architectural heritage were levelled. Three important cities of Nepal, Kathmandu, Bhaktapur and Patan, were destroyed. On the Indian side, the earthquake almost levelled Monghyr (Munger), Darbhanga and Muzaffarpur. The official count of death was about 8000 in Nepal and about 7000 in India, but the unofficial sources put the Indian figure near 25,000.[9]

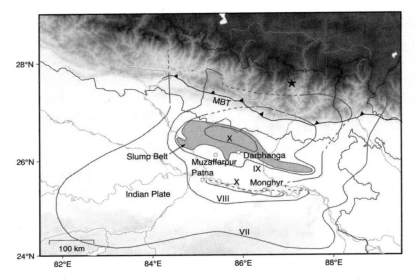

Figure 9.4: Location of the 1934 earthquake and the intensity contours.

Mahatma Gandhi visited Bihar after the 1934 quake and addressed the people. He reportedly said: 'I want you to be superstitious enough to believe with me that the earthquake is a divine chastisement for the great sin we have committed against those whom we describe as Harijans.' These statements are taken from are taken from Marcussen.[10] Gandhi was possibly using this calamity to send a forceful message to his Hindu followers to move away from the horrific social practice of the caste system. Although in agreement with Gandhi on the issue of untouchability, taking umbrage at the irrationality in Gandhi's statement, Rabindranath Tagore challenged his superstitious view. In a letter published in the *Harijan*, an English-language weekly edited by Gandhi, he wrote: 'It has caused me painful surprise to find Mahatma Gandhi accusing those who blindly follow their own social custom of untouchability of having brought down God's vengeance upon certain parts of Bihar, evidently specially selected for His desolating displeasure. It is all the more unfortunate because this kind of unscientific view of things is too readily accepted by a large section of our countrymen . . .'[11] After this opening paragraph, Tagore argued that we should not 'associate ethical principles with cosmic phenomena.'[12] When Tagore made this insightful statement, the science of earthquakes was still in its infancy. It would take three more decades for the principles of plate tectonics to be established as a theory that explains the cause of earthquakes.

When the Earth Turns to Soup

The ruptures of the previous great earthquakes that originate under the Himalayas are known propagate southward and direct their tremendous energy towards the Ganga plains. This style of rupture is particularly dangerous because the alluvial plains contain soft, unconsolidated sand deposits. Alluvial sand can change from solid to liquid form when the earthquake shakes the water-saturated ground. The amplification of energy due to the thick alluvium and the resulting processes were not scientifically explained nor vastly experienced until 1934. The 1934 Nepal–Bihar earthquake demonstrated that a Himalayan earthquake could devastate the Ganga plains in unimaginable ways. The agriculture fields and river valley were subjected to wide fissuring through which water and sand emerged, covering vast swathes of land. None of the engineered structures, including buildings, bridges, railway lines and roads within an area measuring about 2,58,998 sq. km were left intact.

Figure 9.5: Ground failure at Sitamarhi.

The excessive damage at some localities led to a miscalculation of the source of the earthquake. The ground shaking in the alluvial plains of northern Bihar on the Indian side, comprising an area of about 46,600 sq. km, was very severe. The most affected towns of Motihari, Muzaffarpur, Darbhanga and Monghyr (Munger) fell within the 'slump belt', an area of severe liquefaction. Thus, some early observers believed that the earthquake occurred under the Gangetic alluvial plains of Bihar and not in the Himalayas. Contemporary accounts from Nepal describing intensive damage in the eastern districts would have helped solve this puzzle, but these reports (written in Nepalese language)[13] were inaccessible then. It was later learned that in the areas east of Kathmandu, nearly half of the population was killed, and most houses were destroyed. With the collapse of many ancient buildings and temples, Rana described the Nepalese towns of Gorkha and Patan as '*patala*' (Sanskrit word meaning hell).

It would take a few decades before the scientists identified the source of the earthquake. With the advent of plate tectonics, the architecture of the Himalayan plate boundary was becoming clearer. In their seminal paper of 1981, seismologists Leonardo Seeber and John Armbruster proposed a model to explain the mechanism of the 1934-type of earthquakes. They used the idea that the Indian plate is subducting beneath the Eurasian plate, along a low-angle (3–5°) plane of detachment beneath the lesser and sub-Himalayas. Their model suggested that the large and great earthquakes originated on the detachment plain, and the rupture propagated southwards to the Gangetic plain.[14] The researchers knew that any large earthquake that ruptures on the detachment and propagates southward would be like the 1934 earthquake. But history tells us that earthquakes do not always mimic each other. For example, the 2015 Gorkha (Nepal) earthquake (magnitude 7.8) was different, with its rupture extending eastward. One may never know when the next rupture will break southward and extend to the Ganga plains.

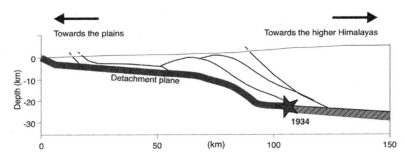

Figure 9.6: Detachment plane under the Himalayas.

Although considered random, earthquakes show a tendency to form temporal and spatial clusters. That is to say, several earthquakes might occur in short periods as clusters. Then there might be a prolonged quiescence. Similarly, they may form clusters in space. Both these trends are observed in the Bihar–Nepal Himalayas. Geological evidence obtained from trenches suggests that a pulse of great earthquakes occurred during the eleventh, thirteenth and fourteenth centuries, and two of them match with the historically reported earthquakes in 1255 and 1344 CE. However, it is not clear whether they originated from the source of the 1934 earthquake. The history of earthquakes in the Bihar–Nepal segment suggests 'busier' periods followed by a quieter phase. The medieval period from the eleventh to fourteenth centuries seems to be one such busy period. And now we are in the calm phase. For how long? We don't know yet, but if the 'winds are gathering for a storm', as some scientists believe, we must be ready and prepared.

* * *

Site Effects and Site Amplification

Earthquake ground motion, which is primarily responsible for the response of the built environment, is controlled by several factors: the source characteristics (how the movement occurred at the source, depth, etc.), distance from the source, direction of propagation and near-surface geology. The elastic properties of near-surface materials and their effect on seismic wave propagation are critical in controlling the damage. As the surface waves spread out and pass through the layers, the structures above starts to shake. Amplitude of the surface waves as they reach the surface is controlled by the mechanical properties of the rocks below, and the most important property is the density which controls the seismic wave velocity. When seismic waves pass from a high-velocity layer (hard rock) to a low-velocity layer (weathered rock, soft soils, etc.), their amplitude and duration increase. This phenomena of site amplification, because of soft sediments overlying hard bedrock, is a well-known problem in engineering seismology. Site amplification at a specific site can be attributed to multiple factors, such as the presence of low-velocity sediment layers, focusing within basins, reverberation of the seismic waves, etc. In cities like Ahmedabad, and those built in the Gangetic plains, the response to distant earthquakes can be amplified, as observed in the past.

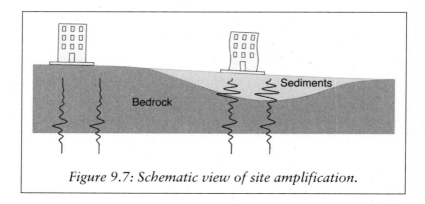

Figure 9.7: Schematic view of site amplification.

Chapter 10

The Trail of Past Earthquakes

Surveying and mapping an archaeological site is an art, verifying the cause of damage is science.
—Nicholas Ambraseys

The documentary *The Walls Came Tumbling Down: Earthquakes in the Holy Land* was aired at the 1991 fall meeting of the American Geophysical Union in San Francisco to a packed audience which included the authors of this book. The documentary was produced by Amos Nur, a professor of geophysics at Stanford University, and directed by Chris MacAskill, one of his former students. The sixty-minute documentary traces the longest continuous historical record of earthquakes that shook the 'Holy Land' spanning 4000 years. For the spellbound audience, the narration was a reality check on the Old Testament writings of doom. The record presented by Nur consisted of historical writings, Biblical descriptions and observations tested against the history of the damaged ancient monuments of the region. Nur walked the audience through the shifted foundations and toppled arches—the ruins of historical earthquakes. The documented record of earthquakes is incomplete in most parts of the world. For the first time, the film brought out the importance of archaeological ruins and ancient monuments in deciphering the tales of past earthquakes.

There is ample evidence to show that disasters like earthquakes often leave a destructive trail in their wake, bringing down centuries-old structures. Countries such as Greece, Italy, Lebanon, India, Japan and China have long records of earthquakes, and the ancient monuments serve as archives of damage information. It was probably Sir John Marshall, who served as the director-general of the Archaeological Survey of India from 1902–28, who, for the first time, followed the archaeological approach to formulate a theory of a great earthquake from the ruins in Taxila (Takshashila). Situated on the eastern shore of the Indus River, an important archaeological site of Buddhist heritage in south-eastern Asia, one of the earliest universities, Taxila, flourished from 600 BCE to 500 CE. The state of ruins must have influenced Marshall to propound the earthquake theory to explain the Taxila ruins.

In his writings, Marshall often refers to a great earthquake in the first century CE, and he writes: 'Taxila was visited by a violent earthquake, which furnishes a notable landmark in the city's history. The effects of its devastating force can still be seen among the excavated remains.'[1] He identified two opposing styles of construction in the pre- and post-earthquake periods. The residents followed stable kinds of construction practices after the earthquake. Marshall's influence was apparent when one of his trainees, Daya Ram Sahni, who later became the director-general of the Indian Archaeological Survey, proposed natural disasters like floods and earthquakes are responsible for the decline of social life in the ancient Indus settlement in Mohenjo-daro. Like Marshall's reference to the 1935 Quetta earthquake that ruined Taxila, Sahni's comment was perhaps motivated by the deleterious effects of the

1819 Kutch earthquake on social and economic activities in the region.[2]

The Ruins Bespeak Earthquakes of Yore

In their book *Apocalypse: Earthquakes, Archaeology and the Wrath of God*, Amos Nur and Dawn Burgess suggest that earthquakes might have played a part in the collapse of ancient civilizations, as with the Bronze Age civilizations in the eastern Mediterranean around 1200 BCE. The Harappan civilization mysteriously disappeared in 1900 BCE, after almost 2000 years of continuous existence. In a special volume on ancient earthquakes published by the Geological Society of America, a team of researchers, including Amos Nur, discuss the footprints of earthquakes in the ruins of the ancient settlements of the Indus Valley.[3]

More than two decades back, while attending a summer school on Active Faulting and Paleoseismology in Luxembourg City, we first met Nicholas Ambraseys, a towering figure in engineering seismology and a pioneer in studies of historical earthquakes. Ambraseys believed that catalogues are insufficient for estimating earthquake probability and one needs to sift through historical records for more information. 'If you were to work on historical earthquakes in India, both of you would be famous, and your work would fill many gaps in the catalogue of Indian earthquakes,' he told us during a lunch meeting. And he went on to add, 'It is not possible to know what will happen in the future, but if you want to estimate likely earthquake hazards, it is necessary to find out what happened in the past and extrapolate from there.'

Ambraseys is right. Extracting and interpreting information from history is challenging, but they help with information about earthquakes from yesteryears. An earthquake often cited as having occurred in the Indus delta region, referred to as the 893 CE Daibul/Debal/Dabil earthquake, is a good example of how catalogues can be contaminated. Ambraseys had found from historical records that an earthquake had occurred in Daibul in Armenia on 28 December 893 CE, but reported wrongly as the Indus delta earthquake. The earthquake was also listed in Oldham's 1893 catalogue, and numerous authors have mistakenly repeated the error, which has now been corrected.

A few months after the Luxembourg meeting, we made our maiden field visit to the Himalayas, accompanied by K.S. Valdiya, a veteran of Himalayan geology. The field trip was from Nainital to Munsiyari, not far from the Milam Glacier, a picturesque route cutting through the various tectonic and geologic domains dotted with ancient temples in the Uttarakhand Himalaya. The rich tradition of building temples in the Himalayan hills may have started more than 1000 years ago. The Katarmal Sun Temple, a ninth-century temple in Almora, dedicated to the Sun God, is one of the oldest temples we visited. This stone temple perched on the hilltop, at an elevation of more than 2100 m above sea level, was built by the Katyuri king, Katarmalla. The steep 3 km climb to the hill is challenging but worth it for the panoramic view of the valley below and the Kosi River that runs through it. On the evening of our visit, the only person around was a young priest who performed the routine offerings. Walking around the main structure surrounded by forty-four smaller temples, we noticed that many decorative stones that were part of the main structure were strewn around, probably from vandalism.

Figure 10.1: The stairs leading to the Katarmal Temple.

It is difficult to determine if the displaced stones are part of human activity or earthquake shaking, as the hilltops are more vulnerable to shaking. Generally, the rotation of individual blocks and pillars, movement of stone blocks and partial collapse of rooftop stones are taken as evidence for earthquake shaking, and that is the kind of evidence we look for. While the displacement of stones at the Katarmal main temple was not conclusive about earthquake motion, the rotation of the pillars of the smaller temples was convincing. Such twisting movements are often the result of a shear motion from earthquakes. The night was falling, and the priest closed the sanctum doors. We walked down the winding and steep stone stairs, thinking of more temples we must visit. We were ready to take the path of archaeoseismology to understand more about the past earthquakes that must have affected the region.

By sheer chance, the 1999 Chamoli earthquake, the first modern-day Himalaya earthquake, allowed us to explore an ancient temple close to the earthquake. This temple was damaged by the 1803 earthquake but it was not affected by the Chamoli earthquake. We were with a team of earthquake engineers from IIT Kanpur led by Sudhir Jain, documenting the structural damage. Located 5 km away from the source of the earthquake was the Gopinath Temple in Gopeshwar, which had sustained only some minor vertical cracks. The temple, standing well over 23 m, was either constructed or reconstructed sometime after the twelfth century, as inscribed on a victory trident in the courtyard ascribed to the Malla King of Nepal. There is a stone inscription on the outer wall (in Devnagari script), stating that the temple was reconstructed after 1803. The visual evidence for its destruction in 1803 is in the form of reused stones, some with original inscriptions placed in disarray. As there is no older record of damage, our initial guess is that for nearly 700 years of its existence, this temple was not affected by an earthquake before 1803.

Another famous temple that was ruined by the 1803 earthquake is the Kashi Vishwanath Temple, a major landmark of Uttarkashi (which used to be known as Barahat). The exact date of the construction of the temple is unknown, but local tradition associates its foundation with the installation of a victory trident between 1050 and 1100 CE. The temple was rebuilt in 1857 by Maharani Khaneti, wife of King Sudarshan Shah, retaining the classical style, but using the stones from the original structure, as evidenced by the misalignment and mismatch between the stone slabs. Captain F.W. Raper, a representative of the British administration who travelled in Garhwal Himalaya between 1807–08, gives a vivid description of the damage to this temple.[4]

Near the village is a curious trisul or trident, the base or pedestal of which is made of copper, in size and shape of a common earthen pot; the shaft is of brass, about twelve feet long, the two lower divisions decagonal, and the upper one spiral. The forks of trident are about six feet in length . . . We had with us two or three men, who could read Nagri, Persian and Sanskrit, but they were unable to decipher a single letter [of the inscription]. The lower part of the inscription bears some resemblance to the Chinese characters . . . The only reason they assign for holding it in reverence is its form being the emblem of one of their deities. It had formerly a temple erected over it, but in the earthquake of 1803, the mansion was thrown down, and wonderful to relate, the pillar escaped without injury.

Damage from the 1803 earthquake was most intense in the Garhwal region, compared to the Kumaun hills on the eastern side. As noted in our 2013 paper, the ancient stone temples of the tenth to twelfth century CE show very little earthquake-inflicted damage, although many of them are in a somewhat dilapidated condition due to ageing and vandalism. We also reported that while several pre-twelfth-century temples show damage from ground motion, the younger temples seem unaffected. In some cases, the documented reconstruction histories have helped to create potential time windows for past earthquakes.[5] Bageshwar Temple on the bank of the Sarayu River is a good case to make this point. As per the records, the temple was constructed during 1592–1602 CE, but it appears that the present structure was built on an earlier foundation. Artefacts of the sixth to seventh and tenth to eleventh centuries obtained from its premises belong to an older generation. Further, an inscription on a stone slab indicates that the land grant from a Katyuri king dates to the eleventh century. The present structure seems structurally intact and free of any damage, which leads to the conclusion that no great earthquake occurred here after 1602 CE.

Qutb Minar as an Earthquake Recorder

Long-standing stone-carved monuments that might have witnessed ground-shaking from large earthquakes are rare in the alluvial plains of northern India. An exception is an 800-year-old tower (72.45 m tall) located in Delhi, which we discuss in detail in our 2013 paper on the response of ancient structures to earthquakes.[6] The tall masonry tower, Qutb Minar, can be ideally considered as a far-field regional recorder of earthquake-induced ground motion. It is logical to argue that evidence of damage (or lack thereof) on such a long-standing structure can be considered central to developing the history of great/large earthquakes affecting this region. The topmost part of this structure, consisting of a plain square top on four stone pillars, toppled during the 1803 earthquake. It also damaged the railings, balconies and the entrance. The cupola (a plain square top on four stone pillars) is reported to have toppled. A remodelled cupola replaced it but was brought down in 1847. We have used the response of this tower as a template to calibrate ground shaking from previous great/large earthquakes, starting with a review of its history.

Inscriptions on the tower show that the construction started in 1198 CE, and the first phase up to the fourth story was completed in 1230 CE. Construction was restarted during the reign of Sultan Firuz Shah (1351–88 CE) when part of the fourth story was rebuilt and the entire fifth story was probably added. A drastic change in architectural style and the type of construction material marks the post-1351/1368 CE construction of the top portion of the tower. There was a change to smooth-surfaced white marble from red sandstone with projecting ribs. Some indeterminate structural deterioration occurred before 1368 CE, and the tower was struck by lightning in 1503, inflicting minor damage, although both did not lead to any major repair.

Figure 10.2 The Qutb Minar.

Ancient earthquakes in the capital

The 1803 earthquake caused minor damage to the Qutb Minar, but there are no reliable reports on any earthquakes that have affected Delhi before that. It is significant that the Moroccan traveller Ibn Battuta, who resided in Delhi from late 1334 to the end of 1341 CE, makes no mention of earthquakes or their impacts like the destruction of buildings during his residence in Delhi.[7] This observation is significant, considering Battuta's penchant for documentation, which included records about a famine that lasted almost seven years in north India and caused deaths, possibly due to plague. As Ibn Battuta had not mentioned the damage to the Qutb Minar, it is a guess that the event that led to the restoration of the fourth story of the tower must have happened after 1341 CE, the year he departed from Delhi. Interestingly, the Newari chronicle from Nepal refers to a large earthquake on the seventh of the waxing moon of the month of *Asvina* NS 464, which also claimed the king's life. This date, based on an indigenous lunar calendar called Nepal *Sambat* (NS), translates to 14 September 1344 CE. The tower had attained its present height (five stories) by 1368 CE. Why the top half of the fourth story was reconstructed in 1368 CE and whether the 1344 earthquake caused any damage is not clear. However, the tower remained intact ever since, until the 1803 earthquake.

Search for the Great Medieval Earthquake

Any discussion on the history of earthquakes in the Himalayas would be incomplete without a mention of the two destructive earthquakes that occurred in 1505, separated by a month. One was near Kabul (6 July) and the other was near the Nepal–Tibet border (5 June) and as they reportedly affected some common areas, there is some confusion in interpretation. Sources such as the *Akbarnama*, an ancient book of medieval Indian history written sometime in 1590–96 and *Baber-nama*, written 100 years earlier, make references to these medieval earthquakes. The *Akbar-nama* describes the Kabul earthquake as follows:

> In the beginning of this year there was a great earthquake in Kabul and its environs. The ramparts of the fort and many buildings in the citadel and city fell down. All the houses in the village of Pemghan fell down and there were three-and-thirty shocks in one day and for a month the earth shook two- or three times day and night. Many persons lost their lives, and between Pemghan and Baktub a piece of ground a stone's throw in breadth separated itself and descended the length of a bowshot and springs burst out from the breach. From Istirghac to Maidān, a distance of six farsangs, [about 24 m] the ground was so contorted that part of it rose as high as an elephant. In the beginning of the earthquake, clouds of dust rose from the tops of the mountains. In the same year there was a great earthquake in India.

These words describe the effect of the great Kabul earthquake of July 1505, but the last sentence about an earthquake in India was an addition. According to Ambraseys and Jackson, who have worked extensively on the historic earthquakes in the region, this last sentence refers to the 5 June 1505 Lo Mustang earthquake, named after its source area near the border between Nepal and Tibet. Quoting Tibetan sources, they reported large-scale destruction reaching all the way across western Tibet. Collapse of buildings and loss of life were also reported from Thakali province (in Nepal), south of Globo. It becomes evident from the work of medieval writers and historians that the earthquake affected Agra, but there are no specific details of any serious damage that support the contention that Agra was 'rebuilt' in 1505 CE. But the lack of reports on damage to ancient structures from the 1505 earthquake/s elsewhere in the Gangetic plains is intriguing, epitomized by the long-standing twelfthth-century structure of the Qutb Minar in Delhi. There was no apparent evidence of reconstruction in the Kathmandu valley either, following the 1505 earthquake. In summary, historical records are not very emphatic on the 5 June 1505 event (calibrated to have a magnitude of more than 8.5) as an earthquake that impacted Nepal or the population centres in the north Indian plains very badly. So, the question as to whether the 5 June 1505 earthquake can be considered as a plate boundary earthquake, rupturing the central Himalayan front, remains open. The next move in the search for medieval earthquakes was to follow the trail of geological evidence that could lend credence to the historically derived information.

Inference of earthquakes from geologic evidence

The greatest challenge for a geologist in search of past earthquakes is to decide where to do the trenching. Trenching itself can be a very involved and exhaustive job, especially if the sites are not accessible by the backhoe for excavations. Following the idea that great earthquakes break through the youngest fault of the Himalayan frontal thrust, the most promising site to find evidence for any previous faulting are the foothills of the Himalayas. One of the trenches excavated near Ramnagar exposed evidence of two earthquakes preserved within the sediment section, as reported in our paper published in 2015.[8]

Based on the carbon dating of the organic samples, we estimated the ages of two earthquakes. One falls in the age range of the seventh and twelfth centuries and another between thirteenth and fourteenth centuries. The older event lacks precise historical affirmation, but the second one may match the 1344 earthquake mentioned in the Newari chronicles.

Figure 10.3: A view of fault excavation in the Himalayan foothill.

The history of previous earthquakes gives us a few important lessons. One such lesson is that a great earthquake in the Himalayas can cause significant damage to the Gangetic plains. The 1803 earthquake, the size of which has been variously calibrated as ranging from magnitudes 7.5 to 8.1) and the moderate damage caused in the distant cities including Delhi is an indication of the power of a central Himalayan earthquake. An earthquake measuring magnitude 8.5, with its multi-fold energy release, can be much more damaging. Historical, archaeological and geological evidence indicates the lack of a large or great earthquake after the fourteenth century. The plate motion continues, and every century adds about 2 m of convergence due to the relentless movement of the Indian tectonic plate. Seismologists equate the prolonged absence of earthquakes to a 'missing slip'. If the stresses are building and if the slip, in the form of great earthquakes, is missing, we must be concerned. And that is why the central seismic gap commands our attention.

* * *

Chapter 11

A Tsunami Wake-Up Call

In the aftermath of the recent wave action in the Indian Ocean, even the archbishop of Canterbury, Dr. Rowan Williamson [sic], proved himself a latter-day Voltairean by whimpering that he could see how this might shake belief in a friendly creator.

—Christopher Hitchens

On the morning of 26 December 2004, ten-year-old Tilly Smith, a resident of the UK, was on the Mai Khao beach in Phuket, Thailand with her mother. Everything looked normal, but suddenly Tilly noticed fizzy bubbles on the water and the waves rolling and thought it was unusual. Soon, she recalled a video about a tsunami in Hawaii that her geography teacher had shown in their class. Tilly gathered the courage to tell her mother a tsunami was about to happen. Her mother had never heard of a tsunami but did not dismiss Tilly. They warned the people and asked them to get off the beach, saving at least 100 people. Another part of the globe, Kanyakumari (Cape Comorin) in south India, where three seas merge at 'Land's End', was crowded with tourists. That morning after Christmas, there were 1300 tourists on the Vivekananda Rock Memorial 500 m across the beach. People on the beach watched the sea withdraw, and it looked as if they could walk to the Vivekananda Rock which was otherwise accessible only by boat. Many even walked seaward to pick shells, fish and other treasures exposed on the ocean floor, and the high waves engulfed them. The Vivekananda Memorial was very crowded, as always, and on that morning, there were about 2000 people on the rock, the *Times of India* reported.[1] The 10–12 m high wave approached the rock, hit the statue and broke off, sparing the lives of the people who were later rescued by local fishermen.

On that fateful morning of 26 December 2004, Chris Chapman, a distinguished seismologist, was on vacation in Ahungalla, Sri Lanka, about 1700 km away from Banda Aceh, where the earthquake originated. As he recounts, he and his wife were finishing breakfast in a hotel overlooking the sea.[2] Chris watched how the 'sea slowly rose a few meters to the level of the hotel's swimming pool and a small wave gently rolled through the pool and the hotel lobby'. He guessed it must be from an earthquake in the Indian Ocean, but he had never seen something like this before. Then the sea gently returned to its previous level, and the hotel staff began to clean up. Everything was beginning to look normal, but the sea continued to retreat for the next twenty minutes or so, and he began to realize that something big was coming. The sea level had dropped about 7 m below normal. He knew then that they were about to witness a tsunami. His wife Lillian alerted the manager, as Chris ran down to get a snapshot of the extended beach without water. All the staff were moved to the higher floors and using a megaphone, they also got many people off the beach. The warning saved many lives.

People on the shores of these two countries had never experienced anything similar in their lifetime or even heard the word 'tsunami'. Those who had heard or read it knew that the Japanese word meant 'large sea waves', but they never considered it was something to worry about. Tsunamis happen so frequently in Japan that the word, meaning harbour wave, was coined by the Japanese ('*tsu*' meaning harbour and '*nami*' meaning wave). Based on the records of the US National Oceanic and Atmospheric Administration (NOAA), on average, two tsunamis cause damage near their sources each year. Tsunamis that cause damage or deaths on distant shores (more than 1000 km away) occur about twice per decade. Globally, tsunamis have been very devastating—Sumatra, Indonesia, December 2004; Tohoku, Japan, 11 March 2011; and Krakatoa, 1883 among them. The story of how the flourishing and beautiful port city of Lisbon, the capital of Portugal, was wiped out by a tsunami is quite chilling. The day was 1 November 1755, and the city was preparing to celebrate All Saints Day. At 9.40 a.m., all the bells of the city began to ring simultaneously, and before people could figure out what the ominous message was about, three major shaking events occurred in the next ten minutes. Most of the churches collapsed, killing the people inside. People fled in the seaport's direction to escape the earthquake's wrath and there they witnessed the incredible sight of the sea having vanished, exposing the sea bed. As they watched in dismay, a 12 m high wave advanced towards them, destroying the entire harbour and washing away thousands of people. Lisbon was a heap of rubble; 70,000 to 1,00,000 of its inhabitants were killed.[3]

The Lisbon disaster sent shock waves into the European intellectual circles, prompting them to question the prevailing doctrine of optimism and the existence of an omni-benevolent God. The French philosopher Voltaire satirized this view and said that humans, the mere pawns in the hands of destiny, have no power in forestalling such tragedies. His contemporary and equally influential, Jean-Jacques Rousseau questioned him and said: 'Most of our physical evils are still our own handiwork. Without departing from your topic of Lisbon, grant that nature had certainly not brought twenty thousand houses of six or seven floors together there and that if the residents of this huge city had been spread out more evenly and housed less densely, the damage would have been much slighter and perhaps nothing at all.' A prediction far ahead of his time, Rousseau warns that the destruction of Lisbon was not an act of God or destiny, but was caused by the lack of city planning and unsafe building practice. The same incredulity and shock prevailed when the disastrous earthquake-triggered tsunami on the morning after Christmas 2004 struck the South Asian coasts, 250 years after the Lisbon event. The Indian Ocean tsunami was huge by any contemporary standards. It was least expected from the eastern part of the Indian Ocean and unfurled into a trans-continental mega-event that left a range of questions to be addressed, from the causative factors to tsunami mitigation measures.

A Day after Christmas 2004—The Tsunami Strikes

The day after Christmas, 26 December 2004, is unforgettable for many around the world. That holiday season was no exception for the favourite coastal tourist destinations along Thailand, Indonesia, Sri Lanka, the Maldives and other islands. On that fateful day, the most powerful earthquake to be recorded in South-east Asia, followed by an unprecedented tsunami, swept through the shores of many Indian Ocean-rim countries. The earthquake of magnitude 9.2 originated off the west coast of Sumatra. Here the eastern part of the Indian plate slides beneath South-east Asia. In plate tectonic jargon, such regions are called subduction zones. The earthquake occurred at a depth of 15–20 km, rupturing more than 1200 km of the plate boundary and displacing trillions of tons of rocks under the sea. The movement displaced many more trillion tons of water and generated a huge tsunami. The killer waves that radiated from the rupture zone slammed into the coastlines of eleven countries from East Africa to Thailand, resulting in about 2,27,898 fatalities, as the International Tsunami Information Centre reported.[4] There were no tsunami warning systems in place for the Indian Ocean rim countries at the time of the 2004 tsunami. Historical records also do not refer to any such experiences. Thus, it is not surprising that community was not prepared to deal with such life-threatening situations.

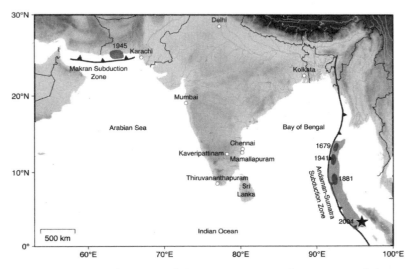

Figure 11.1: The two subduction zones in the vicinity of the India along the Makran and Andaman–Sumatra regions.

The 2004 earthquake challenged researchers and hazard managers alike with its unprecedented magnitude and transoceanic reach. The research community had failed to anticipate such events lurking along the eastern seaboard of India. Nearly two decades have passed, and there has been substantial progress in the science and management of the tsunami hazard. The Indian Tsunami Early Warning Centre (ITEWC)—an in-house unit of the Indian National Centre for Ocean Information Services (INCOIS), has been operational since 2007. Data from the India Meteorological Department (IMD) and 350 global earthquake stations reach INCOIS. Deployment of offshore and deep-ocean tsunami observation systems and real-time data transmission enables the warning system at INCOIS to issue tsunami warnings or alerts for countries bordering the Indian Ocean in about ten minutes.

Tsunami Research in India

We started our work to understand the earthquake potency in the Andaman region in August 2003, almost one and half years before the 2004 tsunami-earthquake struck the area. A moderate earthquake that hit the town of Diglipur at the northern tip of the Andaman group of islands in September 2002 had kindled our interest. The paper concluded, '. . . issue is the lack of a good database on the effects of tsunami waves, to which not only the coast of Andaman-Nicobar is exposed, but also the eastern coast of India—a threat that is generally underestimated'.[5] There was a hint about the hidden threat from tsunamis in this region.

Following the intuition that the region would generate large earthquakes in future, our team at the Centre for Earth Science Studies in Trivandrum took up a project to understand more about the land-level changes along the Andaman and Nicobar Islands. We started GPS surveys in August 2003 in a campaign mode, which means the stations are not permanent, but the readings are taken at the same point occasionally. Casual observation of microatolls[6] above the high-tide level caught our attention, but we could not recognize it as a sign of an impending earthquake. An experienced researcher exposed to the dynamics of subduction zones could have suspected that the stress was building up. We recognized them in hindsight and discussed the importance of such signals in a research paper published after the earthquake.[7]

Coseismic ground level changes are generally associated with many great subduction zone earthquakes. George Plafker, an American geologist, found land-level changes associated with earthquakes in Alaska and Chile in the 1960s. Brian Atwater, a geologist at the United States Geological Survey and a pioneer in tsunami geology research, discovered red cider trees killed by land subsidence in the 1700 CE Cascadia earthquake in north-west United States.

Kerry Sieh, a professor at the California Institute of Technology, and a team of researchers had been monitoring the microatolls to pick up evidence for past earthquakes, taking cues from Alaska and Cascadia. Their study took advantage of the sensitivity of corals to sea-level variations to identify past earthquakes and estimate recurrence patterns. However, the 2004 earthquake occurred while their studies were in progress; it was before they could identify any pre-earthquake process. Despite the missed opportunity, the earthquake gave researchers an impetus to study past earthquakes and tsunamis that might have impacted the region.

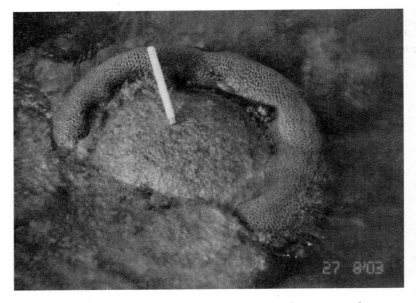

Figure 11.2: Microatoll head at Mundapahar, Port Blair.

Evidence for past tsunami: Archaeological and geologic explorations

As the tsunami washed the coastal strips along the eastern Indian shore, it scoured the beaches and exposed ancient structures that had remained buried. The archaeological survey conducted excavations in Mamallapuram, where the scouring exposed the remains of a temple. During our surveys, we found the first evidence of a tsunami from the distant past within the temple's remains. It was a layer of sand that looked out of place and not part of a usual beach sequence. In the laboratory, we discovered deep marine organisms not usually associated with regular beach deposits. We dated the sand layer with marine organisms as about 1000 years old, the first report of an earlier tsunami that visited the Indian shores prior to the 1881 tsunami.

Next, we surveyed Kaveripattinam (Poompuhar), the celebrated port city of the Chola kings (of the first millennium) on the Tamil Nadu coast. Known to the Roman author and naturalist Pliny the Elder (23–79 CE) as 'Khaberis', this site was a major centre of maritime trade until the tenth century CE. Here, the 2004 tsunami had travelled nearly 1 km inland. Trenches excavated in Kaveripattinam exposed evidence of a previous sea incursion in the form of tsunami deposits of the same vintage as at Mamallapuram. Interestingly, an early South Indian literary work *Manimekhalai*, by a Buddhist poet named Seethalai Saathanar, mentions the 'angry' sea. He writes that the sea 'swallowed' a part of the ancient port city of Kaveripattinam.[8] Could this be an ancient tsunami? Is that the same event that deposited the layer of sand in the trench that we excavated? Some scholars believe that *Manimekhalai* (890 and 950)[9] describes the sea as 'angry', as the sea was rough following a tsunami.

Tsunami deposits are found in faraway shores, but evidence for coseismic land-level changes is restricted to the rupture zone. During the post-earthquake surveys, we mapped the uplift and subsidence of land. We followed the ideas of George Plafker and Brian Atwater to explore subsidence locations in search of evidence of such events in the past. We spotted a line of roots sticking out to the stream at the low tide, about 1 m below the ground. They belonged to a variety of tropical mangrove trees, *Rhizophora*, the most abundant species in these islands. The radiocarbon age of these roots turned out to be about 1000 years, in the same range as the date of the tsunami sand from Mamallapuram. Perhaps, we have been able to nail the predecessor of the 2004 earthquake and the tsunami. More proof was coming.

Around the same time, a team led by Brian Atwater was working in Phra Thong, a barrier island along the hard-hit west coast of Thailand. They provided evidence for at least three previous significant tsunamis in the preceding 2800 years. The youngest one occurred about 550–700 years ago. In a different part of the impacted zone, in the coastal swamps of Sumatra (Meulaboh), Katrin Monecke, a geologist formerly at Kent State University in Ohio, found tsunamigenic deposits dated 780–990 CE. Later investigations revealed more evidence for past tsunamis during the time intervals 770–1040 CE and 1250–1450 CE. These results led to the conclusion that the 2004 tsunami was not the first to have occurred.[10] History of tsunamis around the globe will tell us that none of them can be the last. Perhaps a few hundred years would pass before the story repeats. But we never know. That is the nature of the earth. There are too many unknowns that are at play.

The 2004 tsunami triggered a fresh interest in similar events in the past. Most notable was the 1945 Makran tsunami of Pakistan, which had not created any significant damage in India. Another tsunami from 1881, triggered by a magnitude ~8 earthquake in the Andaman-Nicobar, was too small, 0.9 m in Port Blair and 0.8 m on the east coast of India, as recorded by tide gauges. An earthquake also occurred in the region in 1941, but apparently it did not generate any notable tsunami. The large earthquake of 28 January 1679, from the middle or north Andaman, falls in the same category of non-tsunamigenic earthquakes. Could there be other potential sources? A major earthquake of 2 April 1762 near the Arakan coast of Myanmar is believed to have generated a tsunami that reached the coast of Bengal. However, it is uncertain if the inundation was extensive along the Bengal coast (Bangladesh and West Bengal in India).

Tsunami threat on the west coast: Ibn Battuta witnessed a tsunami

In a previous chapter, we mentioned Ibn Battuta, a medieval traveller from Morocco who was the guest of Muhammad bin Tughluq, the Sultan of Delhi, from 1334–41 CE. He had sailed from Calicut, a flourishing medieval port city of northern Kerala on the south-west coast, via Khambat (Cambay) as the Sultan's ambassador. After much detouring and delay, he reached Calicut in the year 1343 CE (either in June or July), but the rough sea conditions that had developed abruptly obstructed his plan to sail to China. As a result, some ships sunk and others were adrift. The ship Battuta was to board was adrift and had to sail off without him. Ibn's description reproduced here gives the perception of either a tsunami or a storm:

. . . This was in the afternoon of Thursday, and I, myself remained on shore for the purpose of attending the divine service on the Friday. During the night, however, the sea arose, when some of the junks struck upon the shore, and the greatest part of those on board were drowned; and the rest were saved by swimming. Some of the junks too sailed off, and what became of them I know not. The vessel in which the present was stowed, kept on the sea till morning, when it struck the shore and all on board perished, and the wealth was lost. I had, indeed, seen from the shore the Emperor's servants, with El Malik Sambul and Zahir Oddin, prostrating themselves almost distracted; for the terror of the sea was such as not to be got rid of. I myself had remained on shore, having with me my prostration carpet and ten dinars, which had been given me by some holy men. These I kept as a blessing, for the kakam had sailed off with my property and followers. The missionaries of the King of China were on board another junk, which struck upon the shore also. Some of them were saved and brought to land, and afterwards clothed by the Chinese merchants . . .

It is tantalizing to propose that what Ibn Battuta witnessed on the shores of Calicut in the year 1343 was the medieval tsunami inferred to have occurred between 1250 and 1450 CE, based on geological evidence. And, like the 2004 tsunami, it must have reached most of the Indian Ocean rim countries.

The Makran Tsunami of 1945 and Some Unknown Events

The subduction zone along the Makran coast of Pakistan and Iran defines the plate boundary where the Arabian plate subducts beneath the Eurasian plate. The magnitude 8.1 earthquake of 28 November 1945 generated a devastating tsunami that resulted in the loss of life of up to 4000 people in Pakistan (reported by NOAA). The tsunami devastated the nearby coasts of Iran, Oman and reached the western shores of India. There are no other known offshore earthquake sources in the Arabian Sea that could impact India's west coast. However, an incident of a severe sea disturbance off Dabhol (Dabul) on the Konkan coast between Goa and Mumbai stands out in the year 1524 CE.

William Logan, the author of the 1887 *Malabar Manual*, describes the episode in all its terrifying details from a seafarer's angle. At daybreak on 11 or perhaps 21 September 1524, leading a fleet of fourteen ships carrying three thousand people, Vasco da Gama was to witness a sudden sea disturbance when he was sailing to Dabul from

Goa. The waves buffeted the ships and the sailors thought that they were on shoals and tried to lower their boats only find the violent pitching and tossing of their ships by the oncoming waves. The sea disturbance lasted for an hour.[11] The September 1524 incident was a case of 'a dead calm sea' suddenly becoming rough, with no allusion to any sign of previous deterioration of local weather conditions that lasted for an hour. Thus, the reports originated from the Portuguese fleet can be taken only as a description closest to a tsunami, one of its kind reported from the west coast of India. A similar narrative about a disturbance in the sea was reported from the Gulf of Cambay, located ~500 km north of Dabhol. Our investigations could not nail its source. Borrowing the title of the famous book *The Orphan Tsunami of 1700* by Brian Atwater and co-authors, we refer to this tsunami as an orphan of the Arabian Sea.

What Does the Future Hold?

Unlike the east coast of India, the geological records of ancient tsunamis on the west coast are factually less attested. The historically reported incidences are unreliable, but the lack of clarity should not make us complacent. The Makran subduction zone has the potential for a mega-thrust earthquake of magnitude 9 or more. If this happens, the coasts of Iran, Pakistan and Oman, as well as the west coast of India, could face the brunt of a mega-tsunami in the Arabian Sea. That leaves us with many spots to watch: the Andaman–Sumatra, Makran and Myanmar coasts. The Makran threat calls for collaboration between India, Pakistan and the Gulf countries to better understand the potential impact of the cross-border transoceanic phenomenon, leading to better strategies for preparedness. These coasts host critical facilities like nuclear reactors, and many more of such plants are in the planning stage like the one to be built in Jaitapur, near Madban village of Ratnagiri district of Maharashtra, not far from Dabhol, where a tsunami is reported to have occurred in the year 1524. More scientific studies need to be undertaken to verify the status of the faults, reported from the offshore and onshore parts of the area, to know whether they are active or not.

Sometimes earthquakes and tsunamis can trigger more disasters. A classic recent example is that of the 2011 Tōhoku earthquake, which resulted in electrical grid failure and damaged nearly all of the Fukushima power plant's back-up energy sources. The subsequent inability to sufficiently cool the reactors after shutdown compromised containment and resulted in the release of radioactive contaminants into the surrounding environment.[12] Taking a leaf out of the Japanese experience, we thank the forces of nature that the 2004 tsunami inundation near the Kalpakam nuclear reactor had only a partial impact on the plant, precluding a full-blown catastrophe. Next time a disaster strikes us, the lessons learned from our past should stand in good stead. As the geological dictum goes, the past is the key to the future. But the past is easily forgotten. Those who forget history are fated to repeat it.

Tsunami Generation

Tsunamis are generated in the ocean when the entire water column over a significant area is rapidly displaced. The potential energy resulting from this rapid disturbance is balanced with the kinetic energy of the propagating waves. The generation mechanisms of tsunamis are geological events like land- and rockslides, submarine gravity mass flows and earthquakes. Although infrequent, tsunamis are also caused by volcanic eruptions and meteorites that impact the ocean surface. Most tsunamis are caused by tectonic dislocations under the sea caused by shallow focus earthquakes along subduction zones. As the dense oceanic plate subducts beneath the lighter continental plate, their interface forms a trench and results in large faults that are known as interplate thrust or megathrust. Great thrust earthquakes occur on these faults and the vertical displacement on the ocean floor displaces the water column which propagates as the tsunami.

The 26 December 2004 magnitude 9.1 Sumatra-Andaman earthquake occurred along the subduction zone where the oceanic part of the India plate, is being subducted beneath the Burma micro-plate, part of the larger Sunda plate, forming the Sunda trench. The Indian plate moves at a rate of 5 cm per year resulting in the build-up of huge amount of strain at the interface of the plates. As the Indian plate slides down, it sticks to the overlying plate, pulling it down. This coupling of the plates eventually fails, allowing the overhead plate to break loose and spring upwards by several metres. The 2004 earthquake ruptured more than the 1200 km length of the plate boundary and vertically displaced the ocean floor by several metres. The transoceanic waves generated were as high as 30 m at some places and travelled inland for more than 2 km.

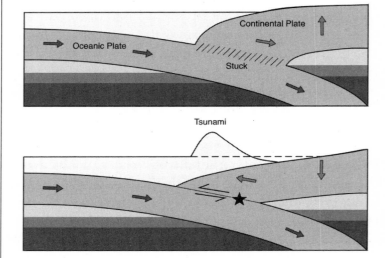

Figure 11.3: Cross-section of a subduction zone before and during a tsunamigenic earthquake.

Chapter 12

Are We Prepared for the Next?

If you know the enemy and know yourself, you need not fear the result of a hundred battles. If you know neither the enemy nor yourself, you will succumb in every battle.
—*Sun Tzu*

Geological events repeat themselves, often over long intervals. As for earthquakes, there are places where earthquakes occur more frequently and their histories foretell that the future will be no different. On the San Andreas fault, one of the best-studied faults in the world, the USGS cautions that 'the threat of earthquakes extends across the entire San Francisco Bay region, and a major quake is likely before 2032'.[1] The agency underlines that its motive is to help people make informed decisions as they continue to prepare for future quakes. The people of California who live above the potent fault line know that an earthquake will happen one day, but they continue to live there. They are dealing with a known danger. As seismologists caution about an impending earthquake in the Himalayas, those in the foothills, and the plains are living in a situation much like the Californians. There are unknown dangers too, that strike like a bolt from the sky at the least expected locations—like the 2004 tsunami and the 1993 Killari earthquake.

The 2004 Andaman–Sumatra earthquake was a surprise because the documented histories of these regions had no references to such events. Very soon, it was known from the archives that tsunamis had visited these shores at least twice during the last 1000 years. One was from the magnitude 7.9 Car Nicobar earthquake, and another was from the 1883 Krakatoa volcanic eruption. But neither of them was devastating. A great earthquake that would rupture more than 1200 km of the plate boundary and create a transoceanic tsunami was not foreseen. The 2011 Tohoku earthquake that created a devastating tsunami and damaged the Fukushima nuclear plant is a more recent example of an underestimated tsunami threat. Researchers had predicted the possibility of earthquakes of magnitude around 7.5 from that segment of the fault, but it turned out to be one of magnitude 9.0. The earthquake caused one of the largest tsunamis in the history of Japan and even damaged the nuclear reactor. In Japan Tsunamis are known enemies, but the power of the 2011 event was underestimated. Such is the nature of the earth. One needs to be aware, alert and prepared.

The Tohoku scenario repeated along the Turkey–Syria border in the early morning hours on 6 February 2023, when an M_w 7.8 earthquake struck the region. Several hours later, as the rescue efforts were still in progress, another quake of M_w 7.7 followed. The shallow focus of the earthquake and the fault's location close to population centres caused unprecedented destruction. Almost the entire building stock of the region was razed to the ground within seconds, killing more than 50,000 people. It will be decades before communities in the affected regions—including in Syria, a country already ravaged by a violent civil war and mass migration—can return to normal, provided the civil strife and military activities don't hamper reconstruction efforts. Two other factors contributed to the quake's severity: first, it occurred in the early hours, when people were asleep, and second, the buildings offered poor resistance to shaking. This wasn't the first time a big earthquake occurred in this region. In 1138 CE, an earthquake with a deadly sequence of aftershocks was reported from near the border town of Aleppo in northern Syria, not far from the recent earthquake source. Given this history, the authorities should have built earthquake-resistant buildings in the region. But this didn't even happen in the quake-affected area in Turkey, which has been politically and administratively more stable as compared to Syria.

The 16 September 2015 earthquake-cum-tsunami that struck the central coast of Chile tells a different story. Chile, as it appears, has learned from global experiences. Following its unique style of construction, it has made commendable progress in earthquake-resistant designs. It is remarkable that for a quake of 8.3, the death toll was limited to thirteen—a proof that improved building codes could save human lives.[2] Compare this with what happened during the 2015 magnitude 7.8 earthquake in Nepal. It released four times less energy than the Chilean event but brought down several buildings, including modern constructions. It killed more than 9000 people, and more than 6,00,000 structures in Kathmandu and other nearby towns were either damaged or destroyed. Nepal's laxity in implementing the building code is a major factor that resulted in the massive death toll.[3]

Let us return to the Indian Himalayas, the smoking gun as far as earthquakes are concerned. A product of millions of years of tectonic movements, its peaks are majestic, but they carry immense tectonic stresses in their bowels, which must be released. The Himalayas, standing in their pristine glory, are a natural wall between Central Asia and the Indian subcontinent. They give us our climate. In winter, they block the cold polar air blowing southwards, keeping India 3° to 8°C warmer than regions of similar cold latitudes in Asia. As the Westerly jet streams blow roughly parallel to the Tibetan highlands, the Himalayas bifurcate these streams into two branches. The southern branch enters north India and gives the much-needed winter rainfall. Had there been no Himalayas, our climate would have been different. The Himalayas were raised to their great heights by the force of the Indian plate pushing up the Eurasian plate. However, their growth is counterbalanced by erosional forces like the movement of glaciers, rainfall and other processes. A dynamic balance exists between the vertical forces that hold the Himalayas up and the opposing erosional forces that wear them down. The increasing human-induced activities in the mountains that include massive constructional projects, beyond the carrying capacity of the ecosystems, would impact the natural course of evolution of the mountainous ecosystems. There is a strong man–nature conflict when humans invade mountains, and the massive collateral loss from future earthquakes is inevitable.

Focus on the Himalayan Earthquakes—The Central Seismic Gap

The Himalayas produced three great earthquakes in the last century alone—1905, 1934 and 1950, but none afterwards. With increasing clarity on the nature of temporal-spatial patterns of earthquakes, there is a consensus about the identifiable gaps along the Himalayas. The central Himalayas are recognized as one such gap, primed for a future large or great earthquake. The long interval of at least 500 years marked by the absence of earthquakes represents a period of missing slip which amounts to the absence of earthquakes that help de-stress the region. A moderate earthquake here or there, like the 1991 Uttarkashi and 1999 Chamoli, is not enough to release the accumulated stresses in the Himalayas. Even the 2015 Nepal earthquake has left the gap unfilled.

The notable historical example of an earthquake from the central Himalayas is the 1803 event in the magnitude range of 7.5. This earthquake not only struck the mountainous regions but also affected far-off locations. It triggered landslides that smothered villages up in the hills, generated distant soil liquefaction, and amplified acceleration in the Ganga alluvial plains. The upper story of the Qutb Minar toppled during that earthquake. Similarly, if an earthquake of magnitude 7.8, like the 1905 Kangra event, were to happen today, the estimated direct losses would be more than 100 billion rupees. More than a hundred thousand lives would be lost. However, if earthquake-resistant provisions are provided for the constructions, the direct losses from ground shaking could be reduced to one-fifth. Such big earthquakes pose serious threats to our monuments in various parts of the Gangetic plain. And Delhi requires special mention as the capital, with many heritage structures, monuments and government buildings.

The north-east Himalayas—an area that witnessed great earthquakes in 1897 and 1950—also hosts such gaps. Further north, the Tibetan region has seen major earthquakes with devastating impacts on the landscape brought about by the earthquake-triggered landslides and flooding. One of the biggest threats in the north-east Himalayas would be landslip-impounded dams and consequent flooding of the downstream sides. The 1950 earthquake of magnitude 8.6 located just south of the McMahon line, the boundary between India and China, dammed the rivers. The dams were breached later, generating flash floods on the downstream sides, and seriously silting the river basins. If a similar event were to take place in the background of the fast-developing super hydro-projects, it would be an unimaginable replay of past destructions. Back in 1950, the vast flood plains of Brahmaputra accommodated the debris. Should it happen in the future, the heavy siltation and giant landslides will severely reduce the water-holding capacity and life expectancy of such dams.

The Last Straw on the Camel's Back

Images from the Himalayas, showing a hectic construction spree, are disconcerting not just from the point of environmental sustainability but also from the point of earthquake response. The unique Himalayan landscape with steep slopes and sharp gradients is not inherently amenable to human engineering as it is dynamically heterogeneous in various natural processes. Human-induced changes to these naturally regulated environmental conditions will likely tip the balance, triggering diverse secondary effects like landslides and rockfalls. Take, for example, the Char Dham project, a road-widening undertaking in the Himalayas. The 900 km long, two-lane highway designed to improve the connectivity to the Char Dham Hindu shrines (Badrinath, Kedarnath, Gangotri and Yamunotri) is deeply worrying from the point of disaster response and mitigation. Due to deforestation and road building, the steep slopes of soft rocks are bound to slide. The proposed 8 m wide freeway will not stand the rigours of landslides, floods and earthquakes, and the secondary effects could be equally severe if not more. The threat is grave when constructions occur in active seismic zones, which may also coincide with areas of high population density. For example, the recent rapid subsidence reported from the hill town of Joshimath has variously been attributed to hasty urbanization, infrastructure and hydropower projects destabilizing the terrain. We must remember that the Himalayan states' population increased 1.5 times between 1971 and 2021. At the same time, there is a three-fold rise in population density due to the changing land use and rapid urbanization in these states.

Another noteworthy point is the non-viability of 'super' dam projects in the Himalayas. Over the past twenty years, China and India have been competing to build massive hydroelectric projects in these areas, which are ecologically sensitive and prone to earthquakes. There are two hydropower projects in plan in Arunachal Pradesh on the tributaries of the Brahmaputra. These are the 600-megawatt (MW) Kameng project on the Bichon and Tenga Rivers and the 2000 MW Subansiri Lower Hydroelectric Project. Across the border, China has already completed eleven out of fifty-five projects that are planned for the Tibetan region. There are about eighty-one large hydropower projects in the unstable Himalayan region on the Indian side (that includes sites in Jammu and Kashmir, Himachal Pradesh, Uttarakhand, Sikkim and Arunachal Pradesh), with another twenty-six reportedly under construction. An alarming 320 additional projects are in the pipeline. These activities are likely to alter the hydrological conditions of the region. From an earthquake hazard point of view, the triggering of earthquakes due to reservoir-induced hydro-mechanical stresses cannot be ruled out.

The disaster that struck Sikkim in the early hours of Wednesday, 4 October 2023, was an eye-opener. An intense surge of floodwaters flowed into the Teesta River in Lachen Valley, washing away several bridges and roads and ramming the Teesta-III Dam in Chungthang in Sikkim, causing part of it to give away. According to the statement issued by the National Disaster Management Authority of India, the flash flood was the result of a cloudburst causing the Lhonak glacial lake, located at 5200 metres above sea level, to overflow the impounding moraine, eventually eroding it to form an outlet.

A glacial lake outburst usually results in more damage and destruction than a flood caused by excess rainfall alone. The incidents of glacial lake outbursts are on the increase in the Himalayas, primarily owing to the upward trend in global warming. It is worth remembering that on 7 February 2021, a similar catastrophic mass flow descended the Rishiganga and Dhauliganga valleys in Chamoli, Uttarakhand, killing more than 200 people and damaging two hydropower projects. The 2013 Kedarnath disaster was another devastating example of a glacial lake outburst caused by the overflowing glacial lake up in the mountain, resulting in 6000 fatalities.

The tragedy that occurred on 22 March 1959, at Vajont Dam, 100 km north of Venice in Italy is an international example that reminds us of the potential threat of such massive, engineered structures in landslide-prone areas. During the initial filling of this 262 m high dam, a landslide caused a mega-tsunami in the lake. The wave of 250 m (820 ft) that formed after overflow in the lake brought massive flooding and destruction to the valley below.

In executing hydroelectric projects in the Himalayas at a maddening pace, the two countries, China and India, overestimate their economic potential. The planners grossly underestimate the loss due to potential environmental hazards, including earthquakes and glacial lake outbursts. If a massive earthquake occurs in this region, the consequent landslips could flood the dam. The recent Sikkim event compels us to step back and reassess the dangers inherent in building massive dams in the Himalayas. The Himalayas require special attention in terms of the potential for earthquakes as well as flood disasters. A special effort needs to be mounted to develop hazard scenarios and models as well as land-zonation maps that demarcate areas prone to floods and landslides. There should also be serious rethinking of the developmental models for the Himalayan states in the context of climate change and the earthquake potential, while also bringing the major stakeholders—the people on board for their feedback and active participation in environmental conservation.

Like any natural process, earthquakes are bound to happen. But the aftermath would depend on our preparedness. Modern and advanced economies are better prepared unless caught entirely off-guard. India must learn from the experiences of countries like Chile, where investment in resilient infrastructure, early warning systems and urban planning have enabled them to survive a massive earthquake with minimum loss. As quoted at the beginning of this chapter, the ancient Chinese military strategist Sun Tzu said in his treatise, *The Art of War*: 'If you know the enemy and know yourself, you need not fear the result of a hundred battles. If you know neither the enemy nor yourself, you will succumb in every battle.' Each of the thirteen chapters of this ancient Chinese military treatise is devoted to different sets of skills or arts related to warfare and how they apply to military strategy and tactics. What Tzu wrote in the context of war applies to the human's effort to combat natural disasters like earthquakes. In a war, each side can strategize, if the strengths and weaknesses are known. But when the fight is with an unknown and powerful enemy, the battle is not easy. In other words, more time and effort are required to win such a battle.

* * *

Chapter 13

The Holy Grail of Earthquake Prediction

There are known knowns—there are things we know
we know. We also know there are known unknowns—
that is to say, we know there are some things we do not
know. But there are also unknown unknowns, the ones
we don't know we don't know.
                                            —*Donald H. Rumsfeld*

Wouldn't it be wonderful if we could predict damaging earthquakes and be forewarned about their time, size and location days or hours before they occur—like we predict cyclones? Every time an earthquake occurs, the scientific community is asked why it can't predict earthquakes as they predict the weather. The advent of technology makes it possible to monitor all the weather-related processes. Still, some of their complex interactions evade numerical modelling and precise predictions, especially events like the onset, duration and strength of monsoons. Every model parameter would fit, and the model would look fine, yet the predictions go haywire. It is a joke that makes the rounds—an Indian monsoon modeller defending himself in a seminar as he quipped: 'It is not the model, but the monsoon that failed'. As of today, there are no models that can predict the time, places and sizes of future earthquakes. Neither their causative factors nor their interactions are observable, unlike atmospheric processes that can be monitored. The long-term causes leading to an earthquake happen tens of kilometres below the earth's surface and none of them measurable. Nor can one observe the earthquake nucleation processes occurring beneath the thick and opaque solid rock. Nature of stress and the faults, their past histories, state of the rocks and other factors decide the onset and size of an earthquake. With none of them observable from the surface, an earthquake prediction model has no reliable inputs.

We must reckon that predicting an earthquake's exact time, size and location so that a warning can be issued is not yet a realizable goal. However, there are ways to estimate the probability of an earthquake occurring in a region over decades, which would improve earthquake preparedness and mitigate damages. Such 'long-term forecasts' rely on statistical models based on the earthquake history of the place and close monitoring of the current seismicity. Knowing the recurrence period or pattern of earthquakes on specific fault lines will also help in long-term forecasting. Scientists have been able to make such forecasts in some parts of the world, such as California. Satellite-based radar imaging of surface deformation prior to an earthquake is a new tool that aids in earthquake forecasting. The combined use of satellite-based measurements and modelling of crustal deformation and fault-specific geological studies have made such forecasts possible, at least in some regions. In summary, the current state of knowledge helps to identify the most likely region of an earthquake disaster. However, obtaining an estimate of the precise timing, location and size of the likely event is beyond the present capabilities.

The devastating 25 April 2015 Nepal earthquake of magnitude (M_w 7.8), the most recent one in the Himalayas, is a good example to appreciate the complex issues involved in the occurrence of earthquakes, even in long-term forecasting. The Nepal segment of the Himalayas has produced large earthquakes in the past. Historical and geological proof exists for a medieval earthquake that occurred in the central segment of the Himalayas. GPS models predict ongoing plate motion of about 2 cm per year. Scientists have long been predicting that a large earthquake is due here. But what happened in 2015 was unexpected. The earthquake occurred to the east of the postulated gap, and the east-directed rupture left it untouched. A large aftershock of magnitude M_w 7.3 on 12 May further east of the initial rupture, was another unexpected happening. A large amount of energy was released by the twin earthquakes, but the 'gap' remained unfilled.

Foreshocks as Harbingers of an Impending Earthquake

The success of earthquake prediction science depends on whether any precursory signals can be captured—years, days or hours before a big earthquake. Foreshocks as potential harbingers of an impending earthquake looked promising after the successful prediction of the 4 February 1975 Hai Cheng (China) earthquake (M_w 7.3). The Hai Cheng prediction was a watershed moment discussed widely in Earth-science literature, and there was hope that the prediction of an earthquake could be possible. The precursory signals included land-level changes in the nearby areas that prompted an initial long-term earthquake warning. A short-term warning was later issued based on the increased foreshock activity. The location of the quake was identified, and evacuation was effectively done. When the earthquake eventually occurred at 7.36 p.m., it killed only about 1000 people, a number that would have been manifold otherwise. American seismologists who had visited the place after the Hai Cheng earthquake agreed that the prediction and evacuation were indeed successful, and there was hope. However, the euphoria of this apparent successful prediction was short-lived. On 28 July the following year, an earthquake (M_w 7.6) occurred in the Tangshan Province, and it could not be predicted. About 2,50,000 people lost their lives. Kelin Wang, the leader of the fact-finding team later commented that the Haicheng success was 'a blend of confusion, empirical analysis, intuitive judgment and good luck'.

Have the scientists made any leaps since the Hai Cheng prediction? Perhaps the most notable attempt is the earthquake prediction programme in Parkfield, California, supported by USGS, which has been reported in many of its publications. With a history of moderate earthquakes with some regularity (about twenty-two years) since 1857, the area was considered favourable for the prediction experiment. Nicknamed the 'Earthquake Capital of the World', the town sitting astride the San Andreas fault was heavily instrumented and was being continuously monitored. Based on the nearly twenty-two-year history of recurrence, the next earthquake was predicted to occur during the time window of 1988–92.

An earthquake of magnitude 4.7 occurred in October 1992, which appeared to be a foreshock. A high-level alert with a seventy-two-hour public warning indicating a 37 per cent chance of a magnitude 6 event was issued. There was palpable excitement about the prediction coming true, and the scientists camped at Parkfield. Sipping coffee at the earthquake café, people awaited the earthquake, perhaps a rare occasion in the history of seismology. But it did not occur. Twelve years beyond the predicted window, there was another quake in 2004, which was not predicted, nor was it preceded by any foreshocks.

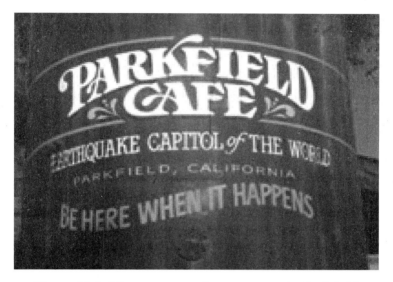

Figure 13.1: The ornamental water tower in Parkfield.

The Quest Continues

Parkfield's experiment may have failed, but the quest goes on. Some scientists think that during the preparatory stages of earthquakes, micro-cracking occurs in the source regions. Electromagnetic emissions of various frequencies are also generated, and these can be used for predictions. It has been observed that large earthquakes activate the neighbouring faults as the regional stress levels are affected. Models of the state of stress provide means to demarcate zones of future earthquakes. While the efforts in earthquake prediction have not been effective, rapid strides in technology will certainly help in forecasting and mitigating natural hazards. Researchers at the University of Texas at Austin used artificial intelligence (AI) to correctly predict 70 per cent of earthquakes a week before they happened during a seven-month trial in China. Although there were a few false alarms, AI successfully predicted fourteen earthquakes within about 320 km of the predicted location, not missing their sizes.[1] We can expect breakthroughs in earthquake forecasting related to some of the world's major subduction zones, with high density of instrumentally recorded data required to develop AI models.

Real-time Earth observation is now possible through satellite-based remote sensing techniques. Computing powers have increased manifold, which makes simulations and predictive models possible. However, we need to be cautious in our optimism because great earthquakes have often occurred without any precursory signals. The February 2010 Chile subduction zone earthquake (M_w 8.6) was precisely captured by real-time GPS stations, but it was not preceded by any typical precursory phenomena. Some recent advances in satellite-based precursory observations augur well for earthquake prediction science. GPS-based data collected during inter-seismic intervals have been used to identify the locales of strain accumulation that may result in earthquakes in future. Some recent studies have shown that many large earthquakes initiate with a precursory phase of slip. However, the current earthquake monitoring instruments lack the necessary coverage and precision to detect the precursory slip at the scale of individual earthquakes. Recent research indicates that the fault zone seems to move two hours before a large earthquake. Capturing this movement called 'aseismic' slip seems to be the holy grail of predicting earthquakes. The magnitude 7.5 earthquake that struck the west coast of Japan on the New Year's Day (2024), which also generated a moderate tsunami, may prove to be an event that may provide some insights into the preparatory phase of big earthquakes. This earthquake is found to be preceded by tens of thousands of small to moderate earthquakes over the past three years, ending with a bang on 1 January 2024. The pre- and post-earthquake satellite images show that the earthquake also resulted in significant uplift of the coastline up to 250 m.[2]

There has been growing interest in the capabilities of AI to detect the kind of weak signals that humans miss. Machine-learning algorithms may be able to analyse vast amounts of data from past earthquakes to look for patterns that help predict future events. Ionospheric perturbations that occur before an earthquake are another signal that scientists hope to capture through satellite-borne experiments. China launched a Seismo-Electromagnetic Satellite (CSES) to monitor the electrical anomalies in the Earth's ionosphere. Some scientists working with China's Earthquake Network's Centre in Beijing claimed that they had found some density perturbations in the ionosphere fifteen days prior to earthquakes that hit the Chinese mainland in May 2021 and January 2022. It is not clear how this occurs, and the claim remains controversial. Scientists at the Max Planck Institute of Animal Behaviour in Germany attempted to log the behaviour of cows, sheep and dogs in earthquake-prone areas of Italy. Some animals are reported to have altered their behaviour when they were near the epicentre of impending tremors and earthquakes. Attempts to use the behaviour of wild and domestic animals, to predict earthquakes, have a long history, mostly in China. The magnitude 7.3, 4 February 1975, Haicheng, China, earthquake was considered to be the only major earthquake ever to have been predicted. Widespread accounts of peculiar animal behaviour and other possible precursors to an earthquake were used in the Haicheng prediction. However, the optimism was short-lived, as another earthquake of magnitude 7.6 occurred on 28 July 1976, a magnitude 7.6, which was not predicted.[3]

Although earthquakes cannot be accurately predicted based on our current capabilities, recognition of their sources, research into their probable return periods and modelling of their effects on ground stability are steps that can minimize the damage. Most deaths in earthquakes are caused by the failure of engineered structures due to ground shaking. For predicting site-specific damage, it is important to know about the severity of ground shaking at each location. Two important pieces of information are required in this effort. One, how often do earthquakes occur in each source and two, how severely the ground shakes in a particular area. For the former piece of information, scientists use instrumental, historical and geological information to create the database. The latter information is obtained from various geo-technical investigations. Information on the ground shaking (which the engineers call the peak ground acceleration) recorded from previous earthquakes is also used. All this data are used to prepare probabilistic seismic hazard maps for different regions, which are useful templates in the design of engineered structures. Such maps are available in India, and their wider circulation and use would be a big step in hazard mitigation.

* * *

Epilogue

Earthquakes don't kill people, but buildings do. The collapse of buildings in earthquakes are not acts of God. All too often nowadays they are acts of criminal negligence.

—*Nicholas Ambraseys*

All statistics show that the risk to humanity from various types of disasters is on the rise. Based on a study by the United Nations (1998 and 2017), climate-related and geophysical disasters (like earthquakes and tsunamis) have killed 1.3 million people and left a further 4.4 billion injured, homeless, displaced or in need of emergency assistance. Studies also show an upward trend in annual losses caused by natural disasters. The underlying reasons are population growth and an increase in population density in vulnerable areas.

During the past few centuries, India has witnessed several disasters, including earthquakes, tsunamis, landslides, floods, cyclones and droughts. Among the various disasters, earthquakes have topped the list of death toll and property loss. The 2004 tsunami was unprecedented, and it hit unprepared nations. Earthquakes from the Himalayas pose a grave danger to the hills where they originate and to the settlements in the alluvial plains in north India. The secondary effects, such as landslides and rockfalls, are also of serious concern. Viewed in the backdrop of the ongoing infrastructure and increased anthropogenic activities, the threat of earthquakes from the Himalayas poses a greater social and economic concern.

Some of these natural hazards have made the communities more prepared. For example, the 1993 Killari (Latur) earthquake alerted government agencies to develop infrastructure and develop a skilled workforce to monitor earthquakes. The network of broadband seismic stations established in peninsular India was a positive fallout. Today, there is a much better monitoring system in place. The 2001 Bhuj event demonstrated that even distant areas could be affected by large earthquakes. Extensive damage in Ahmedabad, 200 km away, demonstrated how seismic energy could be amplified, leading to the collapse of buildings. It also showed how traditional houses were lifesavers. *Dongas*, the traditional Kachhi homes built with grass and mud, survived without a crack, reminding us that it is the buildings that kill people.

The 2004 tsunami was a wake-up call. It alerted the residents about the tsunamigenic sources bordering the oceans along the western and eastern coasts. A Tsunami Warning System is now operational at the Indian National Ocean Information Services in Hyderabad. Equipped with a real-time network of seismic stations, bottom pressure recorders, tide gauges and other facilities, the centre issues timely advisories. There is always a time lag of a few minutes to hours between the occurrence of the earthquake and the arrival of the tsunami, making it possible to benefit from the alerts.

Nature does give occasional warnings about things to come. For example, the great 2011 Tohoku earthquake created a giant tsunami that led to the Fukushima nuclear accident.

Perhaps such a mishap could have been avoided had there been a more thoughtful coastal engineering strategy. The rest of the world, exposed to similar threats, should learn from these experiences. Although tsunamis are infrequent on Indian shores, coastal development must consider the threat of potential future events.

Disaster Mitigation

As most scientists agree, short-term prediction of earthquakes is not a realizable goal, at least for now. However, lessons from earthquakes allow scientists and engineers to predict their effects, particularly the responses of the built environment. Thus, preparing for disaster response is a more pragmatic approach. Applying scientific and technological inputs before, during and after the occurrence of a natural event is a successful strategy. Creating public awareness helps the communities to be prepared. Preparing maps that demarcate areas prone to floods, earthquakes or landslides is the first step in hazard preparedness. Developed nations prone to earthquake disasters prepare scientifically sound land-use maps to educate people about vulnerability. Information on sensitive areas, active helplines and evacuation plans in the event of a disaster help lessen the psychological, social and economic impacts.

Engineering design is the most important step in mitigating damage. Encouraging people to use seismic codes designed to withstand shaking effects is an initial step. These codes, unique to a particular region or country, are prepared based on local seismic activity, building types, construction materials, etc. Indian code IS 1893 specifies seismic designs based on the seismic zonation map of India. Conventional seismic design codes are meant to ensure that the buildings do not collapse under earthquake shaking. However, they may sustain damage due to non-structural as well as weak structural elements.

New technologies, such as base isolation systems and seismic dampers, are available now. The idea of seismic base isolation is to install energy-absorbing devices to 'isolate' the building from the ground. By using structural elements that would substantially decouple the superstructure from its base, the design minimizes the transmission of energy to the superstructure during an earthquake. Seismic dampers are structural elements such as diagonal braces that absorb part of the energy and thus dampen the motion of the building. The base isolation technique was introduced in India after the 1993 Killari earthquake. A school and a shopping complex, both one-storeyed buildings constructed after the earthquake, used rubber base isolators. A four-storey hospital building in Bhuj reconstructed after the 2001 earthquake is another base-isolated structure in India.

There are important lessons from each earthquake that every country must learn from. The currently available engineering know-how gives us the option to follow seismic codes and construct safe houses and buildings. Still, these norms are not always followed. Inadequacies in enforcement and economic considerations could be the reasons for non-compliance. This is not the case with India alone, but it is also true for many other countries. For example, Turkey and Syria, hit by two devastating earthquakes in February 2023, have their own seismic codes, which are not strictly enforced. According to media reports, laxity in practising building codes is reported as the major reason for the huge damage and death toll caused by the Turkey–Syria earthquakes. Take the case of the 6.3 magnitude earthquake that struck about 40 km north-west of Herat in Afghanistan on 7 October 2023, followed by a similar magnitude earthquake, after thirty minutes. Together, the two events left more than 2000 people dead. Post-earthquake surveys noted that most homes in Afghanistan lack a good foundation and are often poorly constructed with heavy roofs that can cave into the structure, making them extremely vulnerable to earthquake-triggered ground shaking.[1]

The 8 September 2023 M_w 6.8 Marrakesh–Safi, Morocco earthquake under the Atlas Mountains also unfurled a similar tragedy. Extensive damage and more than 2400 fatalities—the scale of damage disproportionate to the size of the earthquake—can be ascribed to the poor construction styles followed in the rural areas.[2] As India is going through a major phase of infrastructural expansion in many tectonically sensitive areas like the Himalayas, the north-east, and the Andaman and Nicobar regions, earthquake safety should be of particular concern. Prone to amplification of energy, the north Indian alluvial plains also must receive special attention due to its proximity to the Himalayan seismic belt. It is imperative that all infrastructural projects, including bridges, metro high lines, hospitals, schools and colleges, comply with seismic safety regulations.

Disaster Response and Emergency Management

In the face of disaster, people experience a variety of reactions arising from loss of life, property and an uncertain future. People are generally resilient, and they show their ability to face difficult situations after a natural disaster. However, the support offered by governments, organizations and members of the civil society is critical for the community to recover from the trauma. This is why disaster response and emergency management are considered crucial. Prevention (where possible), mitigation and preparedness matter all-year round, 24x7 for disaster response and emergency management. Preparedness is the community's ability to respond when a disaster occurs, and it is a long-term process. Typically, it should start with creating awareness through hazard education campaigns and offering training to the members of the response teams and concerned citizens.

Response refers to the actions taken to organize rescue operations, evacuate people, conduct search and rescue operations, rehabilitate the people, and provide food and medical assistance. The response is both short-term emergency actions (for example, by the police or the army) and long-term (providing food, shelter and medical assistance), and both these require organization and planning. Where earthquakes lead to secondary effects such as landslides, floods, gas leakages, fires, power breakouts and potential breakout of diseases, the support of the response teams must be available for a longer duration after the earthquake. It is also common for disaster survivors to show signs of depression and stress after exposure, and the response teams must monitor the physical and emotional health of those affected.

Another important and generally ignored aspect is insurance. In advanced countries, insurance companies and financial institutions play a major role in promoting risk education and reduction methods. Perhaps this is built into the idea of 'insurance' because companies themselves stand to gain from such preparation and preventive measures. The implementation of proper insurance plans is not happening in poor and developing countries due to financial considerations, even when there are mandatory requirements. As observed in the February 2023 Turkey earthquake, the huge losses were mostly uncovered by insurance due to poor regulatory laws. In most recent Indian earthquakes, there have been huge losses which the governments partly compensated for. Needless to say, it is a heavy burden on the exchequer. The mandatory implementation of seismic codes and insurance schemes may be a step in the right direction. Government subsidies in the form of tax deductions or even a total exemption can help incentivize insurance for the economically backward. In the long run, this would help people rebuild their lives and homes and not stare at an uncertain future. These are all great ideas for risk reduction, but how do we translate them into action? The answer lies in active collaboration between the vast networks of research institutes, the public and the implementing authorities. The success of all these efforts would depend on educating the people and creating awareness.

In Earth science, it is generally said that understanding the process helps appreciate the outcome. We started this book in the backdrop of plate tectonics, the fundamental process that leads to earthquakes. The Himalayan mountain chain that borders the Indian subcontinent on the west, north and north-east, and the Andaman subduction zone that marks its eastern boundary have all resulted from plate motions. These plate boundaries have generated damaging earthquakes and tsunamis in the past and they will do so in future. Natural disasters cannot be prevented from happening, but we can be prepared for them. And scientific understanding of the processes that lead to earthquakes helps us make informed decisions when faced with such contingencies, both individually and collectively.

* * *

Notes

Preface

1   Kendra Pierre-Louis, 'Americans are missing a key stratum of modern knowledge', *Atlantic*, May 2022.
2   Humberto Basilio, 'Mexico's Biggest Earth Science Festival Draws Crowds', *Eos*, 8 May 2023 (available at https://eos.org/articles/mexicos-biggest-earth-science-festival-draws-crowds).
3   Munyaradzi Makoni, 'Raising hazard awareness at the foot of one of the world's most dangerous volcanoes', PreventionWeb, 16 May 2023 (available at https://www.preventionweb.net/news/raising-hazard-awareness-foot-one-worlds-most-dangerous-volcanoes).
4   Peter N. Swift and Evaristo J. Bonano, 'Geological Disposal of Nuclear Waste in Tuff: Yucca Mountain (USA)', *Elements* 12, no. 4 (2016): 263–68.

Chapter 1: When the Earth Shakes

1   'National Earthquake Information Center (NEIC)', USGS (available at https://www.usgs.gov/programs/earthquake-hazards/national-earthquake-information-center-neic).
2   'Disaster Information: Pakistan: Earthquake: 2005/10/08', Asian Disaster Reduction Centre

(available   at   https://www.adrc.asia/view_disaster_
en.php?NationCode=&Lang=en&Key=897#:~:text=
Pakistan%3A%20Earthquake%3A%202005%2
F10%2F08&text=The%20death%20toll%20has%20
past,was%2090km%20NNE%20of%20Islamabad).

3   Imtiyaz Ali et al., 'Morbidity pattern and impact of
rehabilitative services in Earthquake victims of Kashmir,
India', *International Journal of Health Sciences* 4, no. 1
(2010): 59–67.

4   Brijesh K. Bansal, 'A holistic seismotectonic model
of Delhi region', *Scientific Reports* 11 (2021)
(available at https://www.nature.com/articles/s41598-
021-93291-9).

5   Stephanie Pappas and Livescience, 'Italian Scientists
Sentenced to 6 Years for Earthquake Statements',
Scientific American, 22 October 2012 (available at
https://www.scientificamerican.com/article/italian-
scientists-get/).

Chapter 2: Our Tryst with Earthquakes

1   Arch C. Johnston and Lisa R. Kanter, 'Earthquakes in
Stable Continental Crust', *Scientific American*, 1 March
1990 (available at https://www.scientificamerican.com/
article/earthquakes-in-stable-continental-c/).

2   Sir Charles Lyell (1797–1875) was a Scottish geologist
whose geological discoveries made a revelatory shift
in the understanding of the Earth and its history. Lyell
argued that the formation of the Earth's crust took place
through countless small changes occurring over vast
periods of time, all according to known natural laws.
He proposed that the forces molding the planet today
have operated continuously throughout its history. His

book, *Principles of Geology*, laid the foundations for learning about geological processes. See Charles Lyell, *Principles of Geology*, 11th ed. (New York: Appleton & Co., 1857), p. 834.

3 C. P. Rajendran and Kusala Rajendran, 'Characteristics of Deformation and Past Seismicity Associated with the 1819 Kutch Earthquake, Northwestern India', *Bulletin of the Seismological Society of America* 91, no. 3 (2001): 407–23. This research paper published by the authors of this book narrates the history of past earthquakes in the region of the 1819 Kutch earthquake.

4 K.M. Khattri and A.K. Tyagi, 'Seismicity patterns in the Himalayan plate boundary and identification of the areas of high seismic potential', *Tectnonophysics* 96, issue 3–4 (1983): 281–97 (available at https://doi.org/10.1016/0040-1951(83)90222-6).

5 Roger Bilham, 'Himalayan earthquakes: a review of historical seismicity and early 21st century slip potential', in *Himalayan Tectonics: A Modern Synthesis*, eds P.J. Treloar and M.P. Searle (London: Geological Society, 2019), pp. 423–82 (available at https://www.lyellcollection.org/doi/10.1144/SP483.16).

6 The Global Positioning System (GPS) is a satellite-based radio navigation system owned by the United States government and operated by the United States Space Force. Developed as a defence tool, the GPS technology has widespread applications today. GPS is used to measure the present-day plate motions using changes in positions of observation points, or permanent stations, that receive continuous data. Measurements from instruments that are firmly placed on different tectonic plates record their movement.

7 R.D. Oldham's report not only gives the details of destruction and ground failures from the earthquake

but also provides information on ground accelerations, which reportedly exceeded the Earth's gravitational acceleration. Oldham's account formed the basis for most later studies, including the intensity/magnitude calculations. He also published an isoseismal map identifying a 'hat-shaped' patch covering Shillong and Guwahati with the highest intensity. R. D. Oldham, 'Report on the great earthquake of 12th June 1897', *Memoirs of the Geological Survey of India* 29 (1899): 379.

8   La Touche published more than fifty articles on the geology of India and completed his last article at eighty-one, while living in Cambridge. It was published in 1938, a day after his death. See Roger Bilham, 'Tom La Touche and the Great Assam Earthquake of 12 June 1897: Letters from the Epicenter', *Seismological Research Letters* 79 (2008): 426–37 (available at https://www.academia.edu/23927129/Tom_La_Touche_and_the_Great_Assam_Earthquake_of_12_June_1897_Letters_from_the_Epicenter).

9   Eleonor Marcussen, 'Explaining the 1934 Bihar-Nepal Earthquake: The Role of Science, Astrology, and "Rumours"', in *Historical Disaster Experiences*, ed. G. Schenk (Heidelberg: Springer, 2017), pp. 241–66 (available at: https://link.springer.com/chapter/10.1007/978-3-319-49163-9_12).

10 Leonardo Seeber and John G. Armbruster, 'Great Detachment Earthquakes Along the Himalayan Arc and Long-Term Forecasting', in *Earthquake Prediction: An International Review*, Volume 4, eds. David W. Simpson and Paul G. Richards (Washington, D.C.: American Geophysical Union, 1981), pp. 259–77 (available at http://dx.doi.org/10.1029/ME004p0259).

11 All India Radio speech of Pandit Jawaharlal Nehru, the then Prime Minister of India, in the aftermath of the 1950 Assam earthquake, 9 September 1950 (available at https://www.scribd.com/document/39011483/1950-Assam-EQ-AIR-Nehru-Speech).

12 'Earthquakes', Earthquake Hazards Program, USGS (available at https://www.usgs.gov/programs/earthquake-hazards/earthquakes).

13 W.H. Bakun and A.G. Lindh, 'The Parkfield, California, Earthquake Prediction Experiment', *Science* 229 (1985): 619–24 (available at DOI: 10.1126/science.229.4714.619).

Chapter 3: Theatre of Earth Where the Show Never Stops

1 James Hutton (1726–97): Scottish geologist, chemist, naturalist and originator of one of the fundamental principles of geology—uniformitarianism. Hutton believed that the Earth was perpetually being formed and its history could be determined by understanding how processes such as erosion and sedimentation work in the present day. His ideas and approach to studying the Earth established geology as a proper science.

2 Charles Lyell (1797–1875): Scottish geologist largely responsible for the general acceptance of the view that all features of the Earth's surface are produced by physical, chemical and biological processes through long intervals of geological time. His book, *Principles of Geology*, which explores James Hutton's idea of uniformitarianism, is considered a landmark work in geology. Following Hutton, Lyell introduced the famous maxim, 'The present is the key to the past'.

3   HMS *Beagle*: First launched on the river Thames on 11 May 1820 as a ten-gun brig (a type of sailing vessel with two masts) in the Royal Navy, it was soon after converted into a research vessel. Most famously, the vessel hosted Charles Darwin, the famous evolutionary biologist, on his first expedition around the world. During 1831–36, the Beagle surveyed the coast of South America, and Darwin explored the continent and islands, including the Galápagos, and gathered the evidence that would lead to the theory of evolution.

4   Vice-Admiral Robert Fitzroy FRS (1805–65) was an English officer of the Royal Navy and a naturalist. He was the captain of HMS *Beagle*. FitzRoy was a pioneering meteorologist who made accurate daily weather predictions, and he named them as 'forecasts'. A strongly religious man, he continually resisted Darwin's ideas on the species evolution. Darwin, on the other hand, used these comments to clarify his views about evolution and used them to further his theory of evolution.

5   Darwin's Diary (February–March 1835); Voyage of the *Beagle*.

6   K. Sieh and S. LeVay, *Earth in Turmoil* (W. H. Freeman and Company, 1998), p. 2.

7   A. Atwater et al., 'The Orphan Tsunami of 1700: Japanese Clues to a Parent Earthquake in North America', United States Geological Survey Professional Paper 1707, 2005 (available at https://doi.org/10.3133/pp1707).
    A Pacific Ocean tsunami flooded the Japanese shores in January 1700, but no earthquake had occurred in Japan. The origin of the earthquake remained a mystery until Brian Atwater, a geologist working for the U.S.

Gelogical Survey found evidence for a great earthquake that occurred in the west coast of North America, not documented in history. In their book the authors narrate how they found the 'parent' of the 'orphan tsunami'.

8   The WWSSN, a global network of about 120 seismographs, was established by the U.S. Coast and Geodetic Survey (USC&GS) from 1964 onwards. It arose from a political concerns about nuclear weapon testing after the second world war. The leadership of the three leading nuclear nations (United States, then Soviet Union, the United Kingdom) agreed to ban further testing of nuclear weapons and the global seismographic network was designed to record any such activities.

9   H.H. Hess, 'History of Ocean Basins', *Petrologic Studies: A Volume to Honor A. F. Buddington*, Geological Society of America, Boulder (1962): 599-620.

10 Morgan W. J. 'Rises, trenches, great faults, and crustal blocks', *Journal of Geophysical Research* 73, no. 6 (1968): 1959–82.

11 D. McKenzie and R.L. Parker, 'The North Pacific: An example of tectonics on a sphere', *Nature* 216 (1967): 1276-80.

12 B.L. Isacks et al., 'Seismology and the New Global Tectonics', 1968 (available at https://doi.org/10.1029/JB073i018p05855).

13 John Oliver, a Father of Plate Tectonics, Dies, Columbia Climate School News, https://www.earth.columbia.edu/articles/view/2760

14 F. Vine and D. Matthews, 'Magnetic Anomalies Over Oceanic Ridges', *Nature* 199 (1963): 947–49 (available at https://doi.org/10.1038/199947a0).

15 J.T. Wilson, 'A possible origin of Hawaiian Islands',
    Canadian Journal of Physics 41 (1963): 863–70.

16 J.T. Wilson, 'A new class of faults and their bearing on
    continental drift', *Nature* 207 (1965): 343–47.

17 C. DeMets et al., 'Current plate motions', Geophysical
    Journal International, 1990 (available at https://doi.
    org/10.1111/j.1365-246X.1990.tb06579.x).

18 B. Gutenberg and C. Richter, *Seismicity of the Earth,
    and Associated Phenomena* (Hafner, 1965).

19 M. Barazangi and J. Dorman, 'World seismicity maps
    compiled from ESSA, Coast and Geodetic Survey,
    epicenter data, 1961-1967', *Bulletin of the Seismological
    Society of America* 59, issue 1 (1969): 369–80

20 'Eruption on Barren Island', Earth Observatory
    (available at https://earthobservatory.nasa.gov/images/
    15448/eruption-on-barren-island#:~:text=The%20
    volcano%20on%20Barren%20Island,rock%20
    fragments%2C%20and%20volcanic%20ash).

Chapter 4: Ascent of Earthquake Science

1   Zhang Heng (79–139 CE): Chinese mathematician,
    astronomer and geographer who invented the first
    earthquake-sensing device almost 2000 years ago.
    His seismoscope was apparently cylindrical in shape,
    with eight dragons' heads arranged around its upper
    circumference, each with a ball in its mouth. Below
    were eight frogs, each directly under a dragon's head.
    When an earthquake occurred, a ball dropped and was
    caught by a frog's mouth, generating a sound.

2   Robert Mallet, 'On the Dynamics of Earthquakes; Being
    an Attempt to Reduce Their Observed Phenomena
    to the Known Laws of Wave Motion in Solids and

Fluids', *Transactions of the Royal Irish Academy* 21 (1846): 51–105.

3   Robert Mallet, *Great Neapolitan Earthquake of 1857* (London: Chapman & Hall, 1862).

4   Malcolm E. Barker, *Three Fearful Days: San Francisco Memoirs of the 1906 Earthquake & Fire* (Londonborn Publications, 1998).

5   Myron Fuller, *The New Madrid Earthquake* (Washington: United States Geological Survey, 1912).

Chapter 5: Out of the Blue Events

1   Arch Johnston and Eugene S. Schweig, 'The Enigma of the New Madrid Earthquakes of 1811–1812', *Annual Reviews of Earth and Planetary Science* 24 (1996): 339–84. This paper is about the continental North America's greatest earthquake sequence during 1811–12. The earthquake, the biggest in American history, was not in California, as everyone would expect, but in the central Mississippi valley.

2   C. Demets, et al., 'Geologically current plate motions', *Geophysical Journal International* 181 (2010): 1–80 (available at: doi:10.11.11/j.1365-246X.2009.04491.x).

3   J. Catherine et al., 'Low deformation rate in the Koyna–Warna region, a reservoir triggered earthquake site in west-central stable India', *Journal of Asian Earth Sciences* 97 (2014): 1–9 (available at https://doi.org/10.1016/j.jseaes.2014.10.013).

4   S.K. Jain. et al., 1994, The September 29, 1993, M 6.4 Maharashtra earthquake in Central India, EERI Special Report, EERI Newsletter, 28, 1, 1994.

5   Marjorie Greene et al., 'Overview of the Maharashtra, India Emergency Earthquake Rehabilitation Program',

1999 (available at https://www.iitk.ac.in/nicee/wcee/article/2290.pdf).

6   '1993 Latur earthquake that rocked Maharashtra during Ganesh Chaturthi festival: 25 years on, survivors tell tales of trauma', *Financial* Express, 13 September 2018.

7   S.K. Jain et al., 'Some observations on engineering aspects of the Jabalpur earthquake of May 22, 1997', EERI Special Report, August 1997, p. 8.

8   M. Baumbach et al., 'Study of the foreshocks and aftershocks of the intraplate Latur earthquake of September 30, 1993. India', *Memoirs of the Geological Survey of India* 35 (1994): 33–63.

9   A. Copley et al., 'Active faulting in apparently stable peninsular India: Rift inversion and a Holocene-age great earthquake on the Tapti Fault', *Journal of Geophysical Research: Solid Earth* 119 (2014): 6650–66 (available at doi:10.1002/2014JB011294).

10   H.K. Gupta, *Reservoir Induced Earthquakes* (Elsevier, 1992).

11   D. W. Simpson, 'Triggered earthquakes', *Annual Review of Earth and Planetary Sciences* 14 (1986): 21–42.

Chapter 6: The Mound of God

1   Summarized from an article by C.P. Rajendran, 'The Significance of the 1819 Allah Bund Earthquake, 200 Years on', Wire, 5 June 2019 (available at https://thewire.in/the-sciences/the-significance-of-the-1819-allah-bund-earthquake-200-years-on).

2   The descriptions about the earthquake are summarized from Mac Murdo's report. See J. Mac Murdo, 'Papers relating to the earthquake which occurred in India in 1819', *Philosophical Magazine* 63 (1824): 105–77.

3   Simon Winchester, *Krakatoa: The Day the World Exploded: August 27, 1883* (New York: Harper Collins, 2005), p. 2. A book that explores the legendary explosion of the Krakatoa Volcano and the ensuing tsunami that killed nearly forty thousand people.

4   Charles Lyell, *Principles of Geology*, 11th Ed. (New York: Appleton & Co., 1857), p. 461.

5   Sir Alexander Burnes, British explorer and diplomat (of the same family as the poet Robert Burns), is known for his explorations in what are now Pakistan, Afghanistan, Turkmenistan, Uzbekistan and Iran. For his accomplishments he was knighted in 1839.

6   Alexander Burnes, 'Memoir on the Eastern Branch of the River Indus, giving an Account of the Alterations Produced on It by an Earthquake, also a Theory of the formation of the Rann, and some Conjectures on the Route of Alexander the Great; drawn up in the Years 1827-1828', *Transactions of the Royal Asiatic Society of Great Britain and Ireland* 3 (1835): 550–88.

7   Exodus 14:21.

8   R. Siveright, 'Cutch and the Ran', *Geographical Journal* XXIX (1907): 519–39.

9   R. Bilham and S. Lodi, 'The door knockers of Mansurah: Strong shaking in a region of low perceived seismic risk, Sindh, Pakistan', in M. Sintubin, I.S. Stewart, T.M. Niemi and E. Altunel (eds.), Ancient Earthquakes: Geological Society of America Special Paper 471 (2010): pp. 29–37.

10 R.D. Oldham, 'A Note on the Allah Bund in the Northwest of the Runn of Cutch', *Geological Survey of India Memoirs* 28 (1898): 27–30.

Chapter 7: The Rann Rumbles Again

1   'Preliminary observations on the origin and effects of the January 26 2001 Bhuj (Gujarat India) Earthquake', EERI Special Earthquake Report, April 2001 (available at https://sudhirjain.info/INL_005.pdf).

2   S.K. Jain et al., 'Learning from earthquakes: A field report on structural and geotechnical damages sustained during the 26 January 2001 M7.9 Bhuj earthquake in Western India', 2001 (available at https://www.nicee.org/eqe-iitk/uploads/EQR_Bhuj.pdf).

3   A. Johnston, 'A Major Earthquake Zone on the Mississippi', *Scientific American* 246 (1982): 60–69.

4   M.A. Ellis, American Geophysical Union, Fall Meeting 2001, abstract id. S52G-01

5   For more detailed discussions on earthquakes described in Chapters 5, 6 and 7, the reader may refer to *Earthquakes of the Indian Subcontinent: Seismotectonic Perspectives* (Springer, 2022) by the authors of this book. The book also provides more details about earthquakes discussed in the forthcoming chapters.

Chapter 8: The Rocking North-East

1   K.N Khattri and A.K. Tyagi, 'Seismicity Patterns in the Himalayan Plate Boundary and Identification of the Areas of High Seismic Potential', *Tectonophysics 96* (1983): 281–97.

2   Ruskin Bond (2016), *Earthquake*, Penguin Random House India. This is a short story about the famous earthquake of 12 June 1897, Bond wasn't born then, but this story is about his grandfather and his father was a child when the earthquake occurred.

3 R. Bilham, 'Tom La Touche and the Great Assam Earthquake of 12 June 1897: Letters from the Epicenter', *Seismological Research Letters* 79, no. 3 (2008): 426–37. (Electronic Supplement: Transcriptions of Tom La Touche's letters 1882–1910; a brief biography of La Touche illustrated with contemporary photographs).

4 M. Sweet, Letter to her sister Mrs. Godfrey, 28 June 1897. Small collections, Box 22, Centre of South Asian Studies, Cambridge University. Given by the Reverend J.P.M. Sweet, grandson of May Sweet. Shillong, Assam: 1897.

5 'A missionary account of the great earthquake of 1897 in northeast India', *Proceedings of the Indian History Congress* 65 (2004): 607–15.

6 R.D. Oldham, 'Report on the Great Earthquake of 12th June, 1897', *Memoirs of the Geological Survey of India* 29 (1899): 379.

7 R.N. Iyengar et al., 'Earthquake History of India in Medieval Times', *Indian Journal of History of Science* 34 (1999): 181–237.

8 S.T. Hannay, 'Brief Notice of the Sil-sako or Stone Bridge in Zillah Kamrup', *Journal of the Asiatic Society of Bengal* 20 (1851): 291–94.

9 E.A. Gait, *A History of Assam* (Calcutta: Thacker, Spink & Co., 1906).

10 R. Bilham and P. England, 'Plateau "Pop-up" in the Great 1897 Assam Earthquake', *Nature* 410 (2001): 806–09; P. England and R. Bilham, 'The Shillong Plateau and the Great 1897 Assam Earthquake', *Tectonics* 34: 1792–1812 (available at DOI: 10.1002/2015Tc003902).

11 F. Kingdon-Ward, 'The Assam Earthquake of 1950', *Geographical Journal* 119, no. 2 (Jun., 1953): 169–82.

12 E.P. Gee, 'The Assam Earthquake of 1950', *Journal of the Bombay Natural History Society* 50 (1952): 629–35.

13 M.C. Poddar, 'Preliminary Report of the Assam Earthquake of 15th August, 1950', *Journal of the Geological Society of India* 2 (1952): 11–13.

14 *The Sentinel*, 2 February 2022.

Chapter 9: Events Defining a Gap

1 R. Bilham et al., 'Himalayan Seismic Hazard', *Science* 293 (2001): 1442–44 (available at DOI: 10.1126/science.1062584). The paper recalls that five major earthquakes have visited India in the past decade and how the Bhuj earthquake of 26 January 2001 called attention to the hazards posed by buildings not designed to withstand major but obviously probable earthquakes. The authors present several lines of evidence to show that one or more great earthquakes may be overdue in a large fraction of the Himalaya, threatening millions of people in that region.

2 F.V. Raper, 'Narratives of a survey for the purpose of discovering the resources of the Ganges', *Asiatic Researches* 11 (1810): 446–563.

3 G.R. Chitrakar and M.R. Pandey, 'Historical earthquakes of Nepal', *Journal of Nepal Geological Society* 4 (1986): 7–8.

4 S. Kumar et al., 'Paleoseismological evidence of surface faulting along the northeastern Himalayan front, India: timing, size, and spatial extent of great earthquakes', *Journal of Geophysical Research* 115 (2010): B12422 (available at http://dx.doi.org/10.1029/2009JB006789).

5   C.S. Middlemiss, 'Preliminary account of the Kangra earthquake of 4 April 1905', *Memoirs of the Geological Society of India* 32 (1905): 258–94.

6   N. Ambraseys, 'Reappraisal of north-India earthquakes at the turn of the 20th century', *Current Science* 79 (2000): 1237–50.

7   S. Singh et al., 'The Kinnaur earthquake of January 19, 1975: A field report', Bulletin of the Seismological Society of America 65 (1976): 887–901.

8   M.S. Krishnan, *Current Science*, March 1934.

9   J.A. Dunn et al., 'The Bihar–Nepal Earthquake of 1934', *Memoirs of the Geological Survey of India* 73 (1939).

10 E. Marcussen, 'Explaining the 1934 Bihar-Nepal Earthquake: The Role of Science, Astrology, and "Rumours"', in G. J. Schenk (ed.), *Historical disaster experiences, transcultural research—Heidelberg studies on Asia and Europe in a global context* (2017), pp. 241–66.

11 Rabindranath Tagore, 'The Bihar Earthquake', *Harijan*, 16 February 1934.

12 Ibid.

13 "Nepal ko Mahabukhampa"—"Great Earthquake of Nepal", a book in Nepali, published by Brahma Shumsher Rana, a senior officer of the Nepalese Army in 1935 (Rana, 1935), included many details of destruction.

14 Leonardo Seeber and John Armbruster, 1981.

Chapter 10: The Trail of Past Earthquakes

1   John H. Marshall, *A Guide to Taxila* (4th ed.) (Cambridge: Cambridge University Press, 1960).

2   Rai Bahadur Daya Ram Sahni and John Marshall, '1923-24 Exploration and Research, Northern Circle, Punjab, Harappa', *Annual Report of the Archaeological Survey of India* (1923–24): 52–54.

3   R.L. Kovach et al., 'Earthquakes and civilizations of the Indus Valley: A challenge for archaeoseismology', *Geological Society of America Special Papers* 471 (2010): 119–27.

4   F.V. Raper, 'Narratives of a survey for the purpose of discovering the resources of the Ganges', *Asiat. Res.* 11 (1810): 446–563.

5   C.P. Rajendran et al., 'Archeological and historical database on the medieval earthquakes of the central Himalaya: ambiguities and inferences', *Seismol. Res. Lett.* 87 (2013): 1098–108.

6   Ibid.

7   H. A. R. Gibb, *Ibn Battuta—Travels in Asia and Africa 1325–1354* (New Delhi: Low Price Publications, 2012).

8   C.P. Rajendran et al., 'Medieval pulse of great earthquakes in the central Himalaya: Viewing past activities on the frontal thrust', *Journal of Geophysical Research* 120 (2015): 1623–41.

Chapter 11: A Tsunami Wake-Up Call

1   Tulika Agnihotri, 'Vivekanand Rock saved our lives', *Times of India*, 27 December 2004 (available at https:// timesofindia.indiatimes.com/india/vivekanand-rock-saved-our-lives/articleshow/972712.cms?from=mdr).

2   C. Chapman, 'The Asian Tsunami in Sri Lanka: A Personal Experience', EOS 86 (2005): 3–14 (available at https://agupubs.onlinelibrary.wiley.com/doi/pdf/10.1029/2005EO020003).

3 'Lisbon earthquake of 1755', Britannica (available at https://www.britannica.com/event/Lisbon-earthquake-of-1755).

4 'Indian Ocean Tsunami 2004', International Tsunami Information Centre (available at http://itic.ioc-unesco.org/index.php?option=com_content&view=category&id=1136&Itemid=1373).

5 C. P. Rajendran et al., 'The 13 September 2002 North Andaman (Diglipur) earthquake: an analysis in the context of regional seismicity', Current Science, 84 (2003): 919–24.

6 A microatoll is a circular colony of coral, dead on the top but living around the perimeter. The growth of the microatoll is mostly lateral and they can grow up to six metres in diameter. They act as natural recorders of sea level, which allows the monitoring of sea level changes. Earthquakes often lead to vertical displacement of land and if the microatoll emerges above their survival level, their growth would be arrested.

7 C.P. Rajendran et al., 'The style of crustal deformation and seismic history associated with the 2004 Indian Ocean earthquake: A perspective from the Andaman-Nicobar Islands', Bulletin of the Seismological Society of America 97 (2007): S174–S191, doi: 10.1785/0120050630.

8 (Cantos XXVIII: 1: 80 and XXIX 11:3:25).

9 Manimekhalai is an ancient Tamil literature from South India that reveal references to a sea surge event around 1000 CE that may have affected the town of Pumbuhar (a ~2000-year-old historical port town also known as Kaveripattinam), located on the south-eastern coast of India. Descriptions in Manimekhalai state that part of Kavetripattinam

'swallowed' by the 'angry' (Cantos XXVIII:1:80 and XXIX 11:3:25).

10 Kruawun Jankaew et al., 'Medieval forewarning of the 2004 Indian Ocean tsunami in Thailand', *Nature* 455 (2008): 1228–31 (available at https://www.nature.com/articles/nature07373).

11 William Logan, *Malabar Manual*, 1887

12 'Fukushima Daiichi Accident', World Nuclear Association (available at https://world-nuclear.org/information-library/safety-and-security/safety-of-plants/fukushima-daiichi-accident.aspx).

Chapter 12: Are We Prepared for the Next?

1   'M 7.9 April 18, 1906 San Francisco Earthquake', USGS (available at https://earthquake.usgs.gov/earthquakes/events/ 1906calif/18april/whenagain.php).

2   Austin Elliott, 'Chile keeps having earthquakes', Advancing Earth and Space Sciences, 24 September 2015 (available at https://blogs.agu.org/tremblingearth/2015/09/24/chile-keeps-having-earthquakes/).

3   John P. Rafferty, 'Nepal earthquake of 2015', Britannica (available at https://www.britannica.com/topic/Nepal-earthquake-of-2015).

Chapter 13: The Holy Grail of Earthquake Prediction

1   M. Saad et al., 'Earthquake Forecasting Using Big Data and Artificial Intelligence: A 30-Week Real-Time Case Study in China', *Bulletin of the Seismological Society of America* 113 (2023): 2461–78, doi: https://doi.org/10.1785/0120230031.

2   Samantha Mathewson, 'Japanese earthquake on Jan. 1 shifted coastline over 800 feet, satellite photos show', Space.com, 12 January 2024 (available at https://www. space.com/japan-earthquake-january-2024-shifted-coastline-photos).

3   'Repeating Earthquakes', USGS (available at https:// earthquake.usgs.gov/learn/parkfield/eq_predict.php).

Epilogue

1   'Disaster Risk Reduction in Afghanistan: Status Report 2020. Bangkok, Thailand', United Nations Office for Disaster Risk Reduction, 2020 (available at https://www. undrr.org/media/48520/download?startDownload=true).

2   'Post Event: Marrakesh-Safi Earthquake', GuyCarpenter (available at https://www.guycarp.com/insights/2023/ 09/post-event-morocco-earthquake.html).

Notes on the Figures

Chapter 1: When the Earth Shakes

1.1 Map of India showing important earthquakes of magnitude higher than 5.5 since historic times indicated by scaled circles. The magnitude 9.1 2004 Banda Ache is the largest earthquake (based on data from various published sources).

1.2 (*Top*) A representative seismogram showing P, S and Surface waves. P-wave is the fastest and the first to arrive at a recording station, followed by the S-waves and later by the surface waves. S and Surface waves cause more damage; (*bottom*) hypocentre, epicentre and the fault plane of an earthquake (source: USGS).

Chapter 2: Our Tryst with Earthquakes

2.1 One of the authors with students in front of the Siddha Gufa cave in Nepal during a visit after the 2015 Nepal earthquake (photo credit: C.P. Rajendran).

2.2 The Himalayan plate boundary with major earthquakes during the recent history. The central seismic gap is the segment between the 1905 and 1934 zones that have not been affected by any great earthquakes during the last several centuries.

2.3 Sketch illustrating how the passage of seismic waves causes liquefaction and leads to the formation of a sandblow.

Chapter 3: Theatre of Earth Where the Show Never Stops

3.1 Diagram from an article by Alfred Wegener (1880–1930) on his theory of continental drift, published in *Discovery*, London, 1922. Wegener postulated that the continents had not always occupied their present locations but had moved across the Earth's surface over geological history (source: USGS).

3.2 Map of the earth showing major tectonic plates. The continuous lines are the plate boundaries along which plates move apart. Scaled arrows indicate the direction and magnitude of plate motions. Maximum and mean velocities are 10.4 and 3.7 cm/year respectively (after C. DeMets, R.G. Gordon and P. Vogt, 'Location of the Africa-Australia-India triple junction and motion between the Australian and Indian plates: results from an aeromagnetic investigation of the Central Indian and Carlsberg ridges', *Geophysical Journal International* 119 (1994): 893–930).

3.3 A schematic diagram summarizing the principal features of plate tectonics. Arrows on the lithosphere represent relative motions.

3.4 Worldwide distribution of epicentres of large magnitude earthquakes (mb>4) for the period 1961–67 (modified from M. Barazangi and J. Dorman, 'World seismicity maps compiled from ESSA, Coast and Geodetic Survey, epicenter data, 1961-1967', *Bulletin of the Seismological Society of America* 59, issue 1 (1969): 369–80; copyright: Seismological Society of America).

3.5 Sketches showing relative movements of different types of faults (source: USGS).

3.6 A blind thrust fault that has terminated below the surface forming a fold. It creates a mount like feature on the surface leaving no surface expression of ground break (source: USGS).

3.7 A fault-propagation fold showing how the thrust fault has terminated leading to the formation of a fold (modified from USGS images on faults and folds).

Chapter 4: Ascent of Earthquake Science

4.1 (*Left*) A stream channel offset by the San Andreas fault, Carrizo Plain, central California (photo by Robert E. Wallace); (*right*) a fence, near Point Reyes, California, offset by 2.6 m on the fault during the 1906 earthquake (photo by G.K. Gilbert; source: USGS).

4.2 Figure depicting the 6000 km plus northward journey of the 'India' landmass (Indian plate) before its collision with Asia, a part of the Eurasian tectonic plate. Solid lines indicate present-day continents in the Indian Ocean region. There is no geologic data to determine the exact size and shape of the tectonic plates before their present-day configurations. The dashed outline for the 'India' landmass is given for visual reference only, to show the inferred approximate locations of its interior part in the geologic past. Figure reproduced from USGS (available at https://pubs.usgs.gov/gip/dynamic/himalaya.html).

4.3 Generalized cross-section of the central Himalaya, showing the Main Central Thrust (MCT), Main Boundary Thrust (MBT), Main Frontal Thrust (MFT), south Tibetan detachment (STD) and Indo-Tsangpo suture zone (ITSZ). The detachment plane coincides with the main Himalayan Thrust (MHT) (modified after J. Lavé and J.P. Avouac, 'Fluvial incision and tectonic uplift across the Himalayas of central Nepal', *Journal of Geophysical Research: Solid Earth* 106 (2001): 26561–91).

4.4 The seismic zonation map of India (courtesy: Bureau of Indian Standards, 2002).

4.5 (*Top*) Schematic diagram illustrating the difference between a main shock with aftershocks, (*middle*) a sequences of foreshocks, main shock and aftershocks, and a seismic swarm (source: USGS).

Chapter 5: Out of the Blue Events

5.1 (*Top*) Stress changes and earthquake sequence along, (*bottom*) the plate boundary where the tectonic loading rate is high and in SCR settings, where stress accrues at very slow rates. Earthquakes occur because of fault strength change due to transient stress perturbations such as increase in pore fluid pressure (modified after

C.H. Scholtz, *Mechanics of Earthquakes and Faulting* (Cambridge: Cambridge University Press, 2002)).

5.2 Global distribution of continental intraplate earthquakes (M above 6) shown by black circles (modified after E. Calais et al., 'A new paradigm for large earthquakes in stable continental plate interiors', *Geophysical Research Letters* 43 (2016): 10621–37).

5.3 Map of peninsular India showing earthquakes of magnitude above 6.0. Locations of earthquakes are from various publications.

5.4. Historical seismicity of the region around Killari. Filled circles are historically documented events, and stars are instrumentally located events. The location of Ter is shown by a filled square (after C.P. Rajendran, K. Rajendran and B. John, 'The 1993 Killari (Latur), Central India earthquake: An example of fault reactivation in the Precambrian crust', *Geology* 24 (1996): 651–54).

5.5 Cratons and paleo rifts caused by tectonic movements in the past. The Narmada rift is one of the major mid-continental rifts with spatial correspondence with earthquakes.

5.6 Koyna and Warna Reservoirs and the regions of seismic activity indicated by dotted ovals. The lower panel shows the monthly reservoir levels and frequency of earthquakes during the year 1983. The lower panel is after Kusala Rajendran and C. M. Harish, 'Mechanism of Triggered Seismicity at Koyna: An Evaluation Based on Relocated Earthquakes', *Current Science* 79 (2000): 358–63.

Chapter 6: The Mound of God

6.1 The Rann of Kutch and adjoining regions showing the rift systems, faults and major earthquakes (modified after C.P. Rajendran et al., 'Assessing the previous activity at the source zone of the 2001 Bhuj earthquake based on the near source and distant paleoseismological indicators', *Journal of Geophysical Research* 113 (2008): B05311).

6.2 Allah Bund as viewed from the east from an eroded valley. The scarp is about 3 m high at this place (photo credit: C.P. Rajendran)

6.3 View of the Sindri Fort in 1868, as reproduced by Lyell (1857), has been redrawn (credit: Revathy M.P).

6.4 The ruins of the Vigakot Fort photographed on 16 June 2018, when the author visited the site to commemorate the 100th anniversary of the 1819 earthquake (photo credit: Mahesh Thakkar).

6.5 Photograph showing multiple phases of liquefaction from a section near Vigakot. The white sand layer in the central part is a sand intrusion formed in 1819. Two settlement layers are marked by bricks, pottery, bones and charcoal. The base of the fort, destroyed in 1819, is exposed 1.5 m below the surface (after C.P. Rajendran and K. Rajendran, 'Characteristics of deformation and past seismicity associated with the 1819 Kutch earthquake, northwestern India', *Bulletin of the Seismological Society of America* 91, no. 3 (2001): 407–26).

Chapter 7: The Rann Rumbles Again

7.1 A large sandblow crater formed near Vigakot during the 2001 earthquake, with a BSF commandant watching (photo credit: C.P. Rajendran).

Chapter 8: The Rocking North-east

8.1 Map of the north-east India representing major tectonic features and the three notable earthquakes reported widely in the literature.

8.2 Collapsed bridge outside Shillong, thrown off from its abutments by the earthquake; photograph by La Touche and reproduced in R.D. Oldham, 'Report on the Great Earthquake of 12th June, 1897', *Memoirs of the Geological Survey of India* 29 (1899).

8.3 A sandblow crater formed during the 1897 earthquake (credit: Oldham, 1899).

8.4 A transient lake dammed across the Chedrang River during 1897 earthquake (drawing by Revathy M.P. based on a photograph from Oldham, 1899).

8.5 The hat shape patch of Oldham (1899) overlapped on the isoseismal map of Ambraseys and Bilham. See N. Ambraseys and R. Bilham, 'Re-evaluated intensities for the great Assam earthquake of 12 June 1897, Shillong, India', *Bulletin of the Seismological Society of America* 93, no. 2 (2003): 655–73.

8.6 The Shonga-tser Lake, created after the 1897 earthquake, named 'Madhuri Lake' after it became a location for a Hindi movie featuring the actor Madhuri Dixit (photo credit: Drishya Grishbai).

Chapter 9: Events Defining a Gap

9.1 Location of the Kangra earthquake and the isoseismals on Rossi-Forel scale The epicentre is marked in the highest intensity zone. See C.S. Middlemiss, 'Preliminary account of the Kangra earthquake of 4 April 1905', *Memoirs of the Geological Society of India* 32 (1905): 258–94.

9.2 Barjeshwari Devi Temple Kangra after the 4 April 1905 earthquake. Image by Middlemiss (1910).

9.3 The ninth-century Basheshwar Mahadev Temple at Bajaura, photograph by Middlemiss, May 1905.

9.4 Location of the 1934 earthquake and the intensity contours (Mercalli scale); the star shows the epicentral location (Leonardo Seeber and John G. Armbruster, 'Great Detachment Earthquakes Along the Himalayan Arc and Long-Term Forecasting', in *Earthquake Prediction: An International Review*, Volume 4, eds. David W. Simpson and Paul G. Richards (Washington D.C.: American Geophysical Union, 1981), pp. 259–77).

9.5 Ground failure at Sitamarhi in the 'slump belt' formed during the 1934 earthquake (J. A. Dunn et al., 'The Bihar–Nepal Earthquake of 1934', *Memoirs of the Geological Survey of India* 73 (1939): 391).

9.6 A schematic diagram showing the detachment plane beneath the Himalayas. The 1934 earthquake is believed to have occurred on the basal detachment and the rupture propagated towards the plains (modified after Mugnier et al., 'Structural interpretation of the great earthquakes of the last millennium in the central Himalaya', *Earth Science Review* 127 (2013): 30–47).

9.7 Schematic view of site amplification due to passage of seismic waves. Sites where the sediment thickness is high, the waves are amplified and damage would be more, compared to bedrock sites.

Chapter 10: The Trail of Past Earthquakes

10.1 View of the entrance to the Katarmal Temple at Almora (credit: Revathy M.P).

10.2 View of the Qutb Minar (Delhi), showing dimensions of the different stories and their respective years of construction. The top half of the fourth storey, built in marble, is believed to have been constructed in 1368 CE (after C.P. Rajendran et al., 'Archeological and historical database on the medieval earthquakes of the central Himalaya: ambiguities and inferences', *Seismological Research Letters* 87 (2013): 1098–108).

10.3 Geological evidence for previous faulting is often acquired by excavating trenches across fault zones where recent or historical earthquakes have occurred. The trench shown in the photograph was excavated across the foothills of the Himalayas. Evidence from this trench led to the discovery of a medieval-period earthquake (photo credit: Biju John).

Chapter 11: A Tsunami Wake-Up Call

11.1 Map of India and vicinity showing the two subduction zones (Andaman-Sumatra and Makran) and locations of the 1945 and 2004 earthquakes discussed widely in literature.

11.2 Microatoll head at Mundapahar, Port Blair, August 2003, elevated 10 cm above the high-tide level (photo credit: C.P. Rajendran).

11.3 Cross-section of a subduction zone before and during a tsunamigenic earthquake. Note how the plate interface is stuck and stressed, the continental plate bulging up before the great earthquake. Post-earthquake, there is a relaxation (concept adapted from published literature).

Chapter 13: The Holy Grail of Earthquake Prediction

13.1 The ornamental water tower at Parkfield (source: USGS).

Scan QR code to access the
Penguin Random House India website